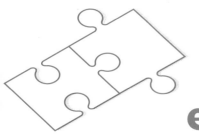

LOUIS FIDGE

essential
English

Book 3

STANLEY THORNES

Acknowledgements

The author and publishers wish to thank the following
for permission to use copyright material.

Excerpt from *The King in the Forest* by Michael Morpurgo and
Creation Stories by Jo Mayled, Wayland Publishers Ltd.

'Flying' by Leslie Norris, Seren, Poetry Wales Press Ltd.

'Dear Mr Merlin' by Moira Andrew © Moira Andrew, first published in
Wizard Poems (ed. John Foster), Oxford University Press, 1991.

Excerpts from *The Lion, the Witch and the Wardrobe* by C.S. Lewis
and *All the Places to Love* by Patricia Maclachlan, HarperCollins Publishers.

Excerpts from *A Necklace of Raindrops* by Joan Aiken,
© Joan Aiken Enterprises Ltd.

Excerpt from the adaptation of *The Wizard of Oz* by Shila Lane
and Marion Kemp, Ward Lock Educational.

Excerpt from *Rainforest* by Helen Cowcher, Scholastic Ltd.

Article on Stingers, from *Bedfordshire on Sunday*, 27 August 1995.

Excerpts from *The Hodgeheg* by Dick King-Smith and
The Nurgla by Harry Secombe, Penguin Books Ltd.

Every effort has been made to trace all the copyright holders,
but if any have been overlooked, the publishers will be pleased
to make the necessary arrangements at the first opportunity.

First published in 1996 by
Stanley Thornes (Publishers) Ltd
Ellenborough House
Wellington Street
Cheltenham GL50 1YW

96 97 98 99 00 / 10 9 8 7 6 5 4 3 2 1

A catalogue record for this book is available from the British Library.

ISBN 0 7487 2540 7

Design and typesetting by Brian Green Associates.
Illustration by Natalie Bould, Claire Boyce, Jeffrey Burn, Tony Dover,
Mandy Lillywhite, Malcolm Livingstone, Darin Mount, Dandi Palmer,
Kay Whiteman and Sue Woollatt

Printed in China

CONTENTS

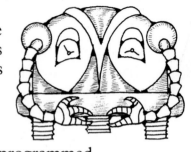

ROBOTS can be any shape or size. They can be tall, short, thin or fat. They can be very simple and plain or they can be very complicated, with lots of switches, buttons and flashing lights. Some robots have long, extending arms and are able to walk. Others move on wheels or on caterpillar tracks.

Sometimes robots are made to look like people, and many are programmed to do the things we do. Some robots can even speak! But they are very different from us in lots of ways. They cannot see, hear, smell, or think by themselves. They can't laugh or cry, or feel any pain because they have no feelings. Someone has to design them and decide what things they will be able to do. Robots are really just machines with computers for brains.

Robots make our lives easier. They are good at doing dirty and difficult jobs, and can work for long hours without getting tired or bored. Some robots work in very dangerous places - at the bottom of the sea and in outer space.

Scientists are making better robots all the time. Perhaps one day every home will have its own robot to tidy bedrooms, wash-up or do anything you tell it to!

COMPREHENSION

● Starting points ●

1 Robots can be any shape or size.

2 All robots can speak.

3 Robots have feelings like us.

4 Robots have computers for brains.

5 Robots don't get tired or bored.

6 Robots are the same as humans.

Read 'Robots' again. Decide if these sentence are 'true' or 'false'. Write your answers in your book.

● Moving on ●

Write the answers to these questions in your book.

1 In what ways are you different from a robot? List some
   things you can do that a robot can't.

2 In what ways are you similar to a robot?

3 What dangerous or dirty jobs could robots do to help us?

4 Can machines 'think'? Explain your answer.

STUDY SKILLS

● Categorising information ●

*Draw a chart like this in your book. List fives types of machine
that are found in each place.*

Machines	
at home	at school

extra

*Choose one of
the machines
from your chart.
Explain what it
does. Write down
some instructions
for using it.*

● Sequencing instructions ●

*These instructions should tell you how to wash a car, but they
have been mixed-up. Write them out in the correct order in your
book.*

Rinse off the soapy water.	Get a bucket and a sponge.
Refill the bucket with clean water.	Dry the car.
Fill the bucket with soapy water.	Clean the car.

extra

*Write some
instructions to tell
a robot how to do
the washing-up.*

5

WORD STUDY

• Syllables •

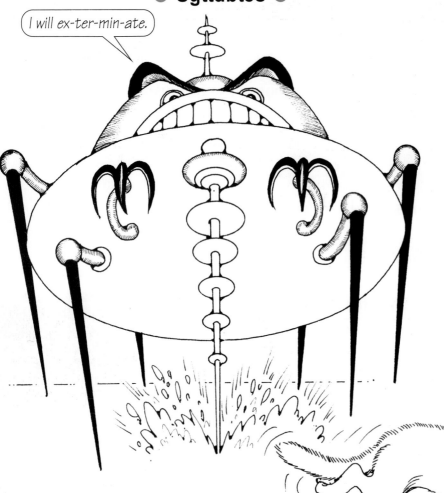

I will ex-ter-min-ate.

When robots talk, they break down words into smaller parts. These parts are called **syllables**. All **syllables** must have at least **one vowel** or a 'y' in them.

*The words below have been broken down into **syllables**. Copy them into your book. Underline the **vowel** in each **syllable**.*

1 ro-bot   2 sim-ple   3 mag-net

4 com-pu-ter   5 fla-shing   6 e-ven

*Now, break these words down into **syllables**. Write in your book like this:*

　　robot = ro-bot　*(They all have just two **syllables**.)*

1 switches   2 buttons   3 people

4 many   5 human   6 message

7 machine   8 doing   9 dirty

10 better

extra

*Break these words down into **syllables**:*
elastic
animals
lemonade
November
hospital
*(They all have three **syllables**.)*

6

LANGUAGE STUDY

I am cooking some zzanklers.

*Robo the robot is very clever but sometimes
he gets words wrong.*

● Nouns ●

*Robo made some mistakes when he wrote these instructions. He
got all the **nouns** wrong. Write what you think they should say
in your book, like this: 1 Read a book.*

1 Read a skxcjjlas.   2 Tidy up the pplwdfva.

3 Cook some qrtaszx.   4 Do the hhjmbxvf.

5 Paint the ggbcjs.   6 Scrub the ffghjkl.

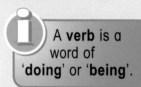

A **noun** is a
'naming word'.
It could be the
name of a person,
place or thing.

● Verbs ●

*Robo got all the **verbs** wrong in these instructions. Write what
you think they should say, like this: 1 Mow the grass.*

1 Snujjle the grass.   2 Mkkffge the broken gate.

3 Wssfgda the car.   4 Klpert the carpet.

5 Mllesft some toast.   6 Ddfwq my homework for me.

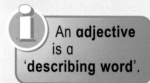

A **verb** is a
word of
'**doing**' or '**being**'.

● Adjectives ●

*Robo got the **adjectives** wrong this time. Write what you think
these instructions should say in your book, in the same way as
before.*

1 Mow the kkjertg grass. 2 Paint the zxghdft shed.

3 Wash the lhnbf dishes. 4 Play some dfghjb music.

5 Carry my snbcv bag.   6 Sharpen my ggvbnm pencil.

An **adjective**
is a
'**describing word**'.

7

WRITING WORKSHOP

● Writing sentences ●

Turn what the robot said into proper sentences, like this:
   robot - bed - made
   The robot made the bed.
Then, copy the sentences into your book.

Robot - bed - made

1 football - boy - window

2 tree - wind - blew down

3 milk - cat - table

4 bike - flat tyre - puncture

5 hedgehog - woods - garden

6 thief - car - stole

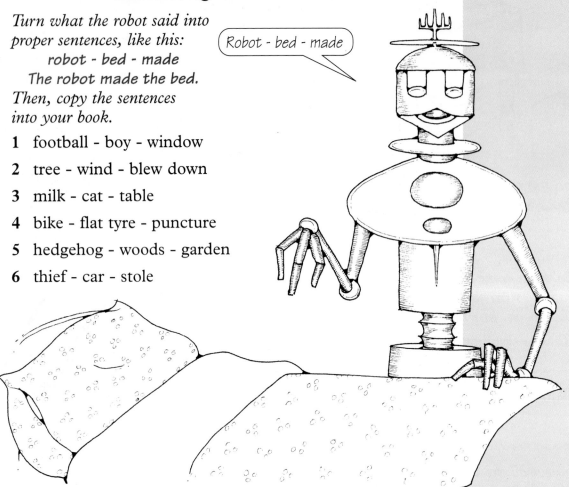

● Muddled endings ●

When Robo speaks he misses out some words and muddles up others.
Match the beginnings of these sentences to the correct endings.
Write the complete sentences in your book.

1 The robot fried an egg **up the flagpole**.

2 The girl is putting her gloves **on his head**.

3 The boy spread some jam **on her hands**.

4 The man wears his hat **on his toast**.

5 The flag is flying **in the pan**.

Labelling and
● writing accurate descriptions ●

This robot has some special features. The lines point to them.
Make up some labels for the features and write them in your
book. The first three have been done for you.

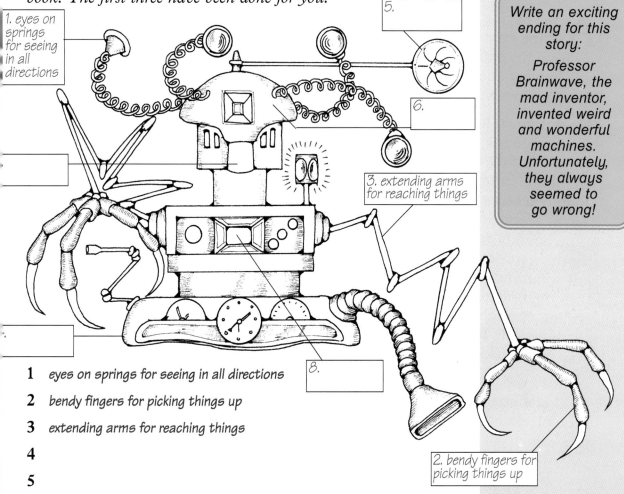

1. eyes on springs for seeing in all directions

5.

6.

3. extending arms for reaching things

8.

2. bendy fingers for picking things up

extra

Write an exciting ending for this story:

Professor Brainwave, the mad inventor, invented weird and wonderful machines. Unfortunately, they always seemed to go wrong!

1 eyes on springs for seeing in all directions

2 bendy fingers for picking things up

3 extending arms for reaching things

4

5

6

7

8

● My very own robot ●

- *Draw a large picture of a robot in your book.*
- *Add some special features.*
- *Label all the parts.*
- *Write at least five sentences about your robot. Explain what it can do.*

When you have finished any piece of writing, read it through slowly. Can you find any ways of improving it? Check your writing for silly mistakes.

The king of the forest

As the baying of the hounds came ever closer, Tod looked up from his chopping. Something was moving at the edge of the forest, something white and small.

He put down his axe and ran over to see what it was, and there trembling in the high bracken was a fawn, a white fawn. The hounds and the horns were sounding all about him now, and he could see the huntsmen riding through the trees. Swiftly he gathered the fawn in his arms and ran back inside the cottage.

Once inside he jumped into bed, still cradling the fawn, and pulled the blanket up over his nose.

He lay there and held his breath. Outside he could hear the horses snorting and pawing the ground.

Then the hounds were whining and scratching at the door. Beside him he could feel the fawn panting under his hand.

Suddenly the door was thrown open, and the King was standing there all muddy from the chase. He came into the room, the huntsmen behind him.

"We were hunting the white fawn, boy," he said. "The hounds led us here to your cottage door." He was looking round the room.

"I am not well," said Tod, the blanket still over his nose. "I have been in bed all day and have seen nothing Sire." *Michael Murpurgo*

COMPREHENSION

● Starting points ●

Answer these questions in your book.

1 What did Tod hear coming closer?

2 What were the huntsmen chasing?

3 Where did Tod live?

4 Why did Tod hide the fawn in his bed?

5 What important person was out hunting?

6 What lie did Tod tell?

● Moving on ●

Now, answer these questions.

1 How can you tell that the story took place in the past?

2 How do you think Tod felt when the huntsmen came into his cottage?

3 Was Tod right to lie to the King? Explain your answer.

STUDY SKILLS

● Using context clues ●

Work out what each of the underlined words means.

1 The old house was delapidated and needed a lot of repairs.
   a) made of wood   **b**) falling to pieces   **c**) very important

2 In olden days, people illuminated their houses with candles.
   a) cleaned   **b**) painted   **c**) lit up

3 The poor old woman was dressed in dowdy clothes.
   a) expensive   **b**) shabby   **c**) smart

4 After all the sunshine, the land was parched.
   a) very dry   **b**) green   **c**) good for farming

i We can often work out the meaning of a difficult word by looking for clues in the rest of the sentence (the **context**).

● Book blurbs ●

Read this **'book blurb'**.

> Sam and Shiva decide to look for adventure on holiday. They certainly find it! They manage to trap a burglar, prevent a car theft and uncover a forger - but not without a few narrow escapes! Join them in their adventures, and be prepared to be scared!

• *Make up a good title for the book.*
• *Does the* **'blurb'** *make you want to read the book? Explain your answer.*
• *Make up a* **'book blurb'** *for 'The king of the forest'. Write it in your book.*

i 'Book blurb' gives a short description of what a book is about. The 'blurb' is often written on the back cover.

extra

Design an exciting book cover for 'The king of the forest'.

11

WORD STUDY

● Words ending in 'le' and 'el' ●

Find all the words that end with 'le' and 'el' in the wordsearch.
Write them in your book.

I'm hunting for words ending in 'le' and 'el'. There are five of each hiding in the puzzle.

a	b	c	d	c	a	n	d	l	e
e	s	i	m	p	l	e	f	g	h
i	j	c	a	m	e	l	k	l	m
n	o	t	r	e	m	b	l	e	p
a	n	k	l	e	q	r	s	t	u
v	w	x	y	z	v	o	w	e	l
a	t	r	a	v	e	l	b	c	d
e	f	g	j	e	w	e	l	h	i
l	a	b	e	l	j	k	s	m	n
o	p	g	r	u	m	b	l	e	q

extra

Think of three more words that end with 'le' and 'el'. Write them in your book.

● Words ending in 'al' and 'il' ●

Copy these beginnings of words into your book. Finish them with either 'al' or 'il'.

1 penc _ _   2 tot _ _   3 anim _ _

4 Apr _ _   5 pup _ _   6 unt _ _

7 decim _ _   8 sever _ _   9 usu _ _

10 foss _ _   11 daffod _ _   12 sign _ _

i Use a dictionary to check your answers.

extra

Make up six sentences with 'il' and 'al' words in them.

12

LANGUAGE STUDY

● Verb tenses - past, present and future. ●

Last week I <u>played</u> football.

Today I <u>am playing</u> tennis.

Next week I <u>will play</u> netball.

ℹ️ We change the way we write **verbs** according to whether things happen in the **past**, **present** or **future**.

This happened in the past, so the verb is written in the **past** tense.

This is happening in the present (now), so the verb is written in the **present** tense.

This will happen in the future, so the verb is written in the **future** tense.

*Copy these sentences into your book. Underline the **verb** in each one, and say whether it is written in the **past**, **present** or **future tense**. The first one has been done for you.*

1 In the summer, I <u>will get</u> a new bike.

(future tense)

2 Many years ago, Tod lived in the forest.

3 Marie is eating a sweet.

4 Next week, Shanaz is going on holiday.

5 Yesterday, we sailed our boats on the river.

6 I feel ill.

extra

Make up some sentences using these phrases.

last week
next Saturday
tomorrow
at the moment
now
many years ago
when I grow up
yesterday
when I was a baby
in a hundred years
next week

*Underline the **verb** in each sentence. Say whether the sentences are written in the **past**, **present** or **future tense**.*

WRITING WORKSHOP

● Thinking about stories ●

This 'ladder' can help you to plan stories. Read the information on the 'ladder', starting at STEP 1.

STEP 4 - STORY-LINE/PLOT

Beginning of story:
• How will it begin?
• How can you make it interesting?

Middle of story:
• What sort of things do you want to happen?

Story ending
• What sort of ending will your story have?
(Will it be happy? sad? exciting? interesting?)

STEP 3 - CHARACTERS

Who will the main characters be?
They could be:
• humans
• animals
• Other things (like robots, space creatures etc)

What would you like them to:
• look like?
• be like?

STEP 2 - SETTING

When will the story take place?
It could be set in the:
• present
• future (in time to come)
• past (in time gone by).

Where will it take place?
It could be set in:
• a real place (like a house or a tent)
• an imaginary place (like a spooky castle or forest).

STEP 1 - TYPE OF STORY

What type of story will it be?
Here are some types of story:
• adventure • animal • funny
• frightening • fantasy.

AUDIENCE
You also need to think about who you are writing the story for. Is it just for you, your friends, younger children, older people? You can write stories for people you have never met.

● Thinking about 'The king of the forest' ●

Read 'The king of the forest' (on page 10) again. Write the answers to these questions in your book.

1 What **type of story** do you think it is?
   a) a war story **b**) a horror story **c**) a fairy story
   d) an adventure story **e**) a space story

2 Think about the **setting**. When does the story take place?
   a) in the present **b**) in the future **c**) in the past

3 Where does it take place?
   a) in a town **b**) in a forest **c**) by a lake

4 What do you think Tod's cottage was like? Write a description of it.

5 Think about the **characters**. What do you think Tod was like? Was he poor, selfish, kind, brave, foolish, a liar?

6 Think about the **plot** of 'The king of the forest'. What do you think will happen to Tod and the fawn? Will the story have a happy or sad ending? Write an exciting ending for 'The king of the forest'.

● Feelings ●

What makes you worried:

being lost?

people who shout?

shadows at night?

Write about a time when you were really worried.
• *What worried you?* • *Who was involved?* • *Where were you?*
• *What happened?* • *How did it end?*

15

THE family had crowded round him on his return, all talking at once.

"Where have you been all this time?" asked Ma.

"Are you all right, son?" asked Pa.

"Did you cross the road?" they both said, and Peony, Pansy and Petunia echoed, "Did you? Did you? Did you?"

For a while Max did not reply. His thoughts were all muddled, and when he did speak, his words were muddled too. "I got a head on the bump," he said slowly. The family looked at one another. "Something bot me on the hittom," said Max, "and then I headed my bang. My ache bads headly."

"But did you cross the road?" cried his sisters.

"Yes," said Max wearily. "I hound where the fumans cross over, but..."

"But the traffic stops only if you're human?" interrupted Pa.

"Yes," said Max. "Not if you're a hodgeheg."

Dick King-Smith

COMPREHENSION

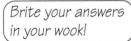

Brite your answers in your wook!

● Starting points ●

1 What are the names of the characters in the story?

2 What did everyone want to know?

3 Where did Max have a bump?

4 How can you tell Max is all muddled?

● Moving on ●

Now, answer these questions in your book.

1 Why was everyone so concerned about Max?

2 Why do you think Max was all muddled up?

3 What part of the road do you think Max tried to cross? Explain your answer.

STUDY SKILLS

● Alphabetical order and definitions ●

*Write these words in your book in **alphabetical order**, according to their third letters.*

hollow   hobby   hospital   honest

*Choose the correct **definition** to go with each of the words above. Write each word alongside its **definition** in your book.*

1 something you do in your spare time
2 empty
3 always truthful
4 a building for people who are ill or hurt

*Now, write these words in **alphabetical order**, according to their fourth letters.*

cross   crowd   crop   croak

*Choose the correct **definition** to go with each of the words above. Copy them into your book in the same way as before.*

1 angry
2 plants grown for food
3 the noise a frog makes
4 a lot of people

● Writing names in alphabetical order ●

*Write these names in **alphabetical order**, according to the first letters of the surnames.*

1 Vasco de Gama   Ferdinand Magellan
   Francis Drake   Walter Raleigh
   Thor Heyerdahl   Christopher Columbus

2 Vicky Smith
   Matthew Day
   Ali Esfandary
   Shanaz Riaz
   Shiva Patel
   Sara Hill

Help me to sort these names into alphabetical order!

extra

Find a reference book about hedgehogs. Write five interesting facts about hedgehogs in your book.

Use a dictionary to check the meanings of any words you don't know.

When you look up peoples' names in reference books, they are arranged in order according to their surnames. (Be careful though, in some countries surnames are always written first, e.g. in China.)

WORD STUDY

● 'dge' words ●

*Help me to find out where the **vowels** go!*

Choose a vowel (**a, e, i, o** or **u**) to finish each word. Write the words in your book.

1	br _ dge	2	h _ dge	3	d _ dge
4	f _ dge	5	w _ dge	6	b _ dger
7	fr _ dge	8	l _ dger	9	tr _ dge
10	b _ dget	11	m _ dge	12	sl _ dge

Now, copy this chart into your book. Write the '**dge**' words that you have made in the correct columns.

-adge	-edge	-idge	-odge	-udge
	hedge	bridge		

● Changing words ●

Follow these instructions.
Write the new words in your book.

1 Change the '**d**' in **d**itch to:
   a) h   **b)** p   **c)** st   **d)** w

2 Change the '**b**' in **b**atch to:
   a) c   **b)** m   **c)** w   **d)** th

If I change the first letters of words, I can make new words!

extra

*Can you think of any words that end in '**etch**' or '**utch**'?*

18

LANGUAGE STUDY

● Standard English ●

*Write down what these people are saying in **Standard English**.
The first one has been done for you.*

Go away! I don't want to play with you.

● Cockney rhyming slang ●

*Match the **phrases** in '**rhyming slang**' to their meanings.*

dog and bone	boots
apples and pears	mouth
plates of meat	telephone
mince pies	road
north and south	stairs
Barnet Fair	eyes
daisy roots	feet
frog and toad	hair

When we're talking, we often use **non-Standard English**. This means that we say things differently from the way we would write them. When we want to write something down so that everyone can understand it, we use **Standard English**.

People called Cockneys - who live in a particular area of London - often say things in '**rhyming slang**'.
e.g. **dog and bone** means **telephone**.

19

WRITING WORKSHOP

● Mixed-up words ●

Ladles and Jellyspoons:
I come before you
To stand behind you
And tell you something
I know nothing about.

'Ladles and jellyspoons' is a funny way of saying 'ladies and gentlemen'.

Think of pairs of words that go together. Write them in your book. Have fun swapping their first letters around, like this.

cups and saucers	-	sups and caucers
tables and chairs	-	chables and tairs
frogs and toads	-	trogs and foads
cats and dogs	-	dats and cogs

Make up a silly poem using your pairs of words.

● The hedgehog's nonsense poem ●

The hedgehog's poem

One day I saw a hedgehog knitting a jumper
I saw an old lady made of cardboard
I saw a box talking to a policeman
I saw a girl chewing a bone
I saw a dog seated on the throne
I saw a king playing table tennis
I saw some children.

Rewrite 'The hedgehog's poem' so that it makes sense.
Punctuate it correctly. The first two lines have been done for you:
    One day I saw a hedgehog.
    Knitting a jumper, I saw an old lady

extra

Say this tongue-twister as fast as you can:

Swan swam in the sea,
Swim, swan, swim!
Swan swam back again,
Well swum, swan!

20

● Writing an animal adventure story ●

Use these ideas to help you plan and write an animal adventure story.

MAIN CHARACTER

- Imagine that you are an animal that lives in a wood. You could be a rabbit, hedgehog, fox or other type of animal.
  - What's your name?
  - What do you look like?
  - What habits have you got?
  - What sort of things do you like doing? Do you like playing with friends, hunting for food or spending time with your family?

SETTING

- Where do you live - in a burrow, hollow tree underground or somewhere else?
- What is the wood like that you live in?
- Who do you live with?

PLOT

Beginning

- Imagine that something happens to make you leave home:
- Do you have to go on a long journey to see relatives?
- Do you have to move to a bigger house?
- Is there a disaster, like a fire or flood?
- Does something else awful happen?

Middle

- While you are out in the world, you have an adventure. Perhaps you:
  - see humans for the first time (What do they look like? How do they behave?)
  - see cars and have to cross a road
  - meet an enemy
  - are chased and captured. (Remember to write about what you see, smell, hear, do, feel, say.)

Ending

- How will your story end? Think of an interesting or unusual way to end it.

Flying

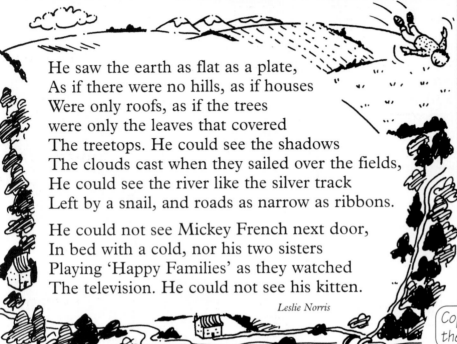

He saw the earth as flat as a plate,
As if there were no hills, as if houses
Were only roofs, as if the trees
were only the leaves that covered
The treetops. He could see the shadows
The clouds cast when they sailed over the fields,
He could see the river like the silver track
Left by a snail, and roads as narrow as ribbons.

He could not see Mickey French next door,
In bed with a cold, nor his two sisters
Playing 'Happy Families' as they watched
The television. He could not see his kitten.

Leslie Norris

Copy and complete these sentences.

COMPREHENSION

● Starting points ●

1 The earth looked as flat...

2 The river was like the...

3 The roads were as narrow...

4 Mickey French was in bed...

5 His two sisters were...

6 He could not see his...

● Moving on ●

Write the answers to these questions in your book.

1 Why do you think it looked as if the houses were only roofs?

2 Why do you think the roads looked as narrow as ribbons?

3 Why do you think 'he' couldn't see Mickey French?

4 What things do you think you might see if you flew over your school right now? List them in your book.

extra

Think of as many things as you can that fly. List them in your book.

STUDY SKILLS

● Maps and plans ●

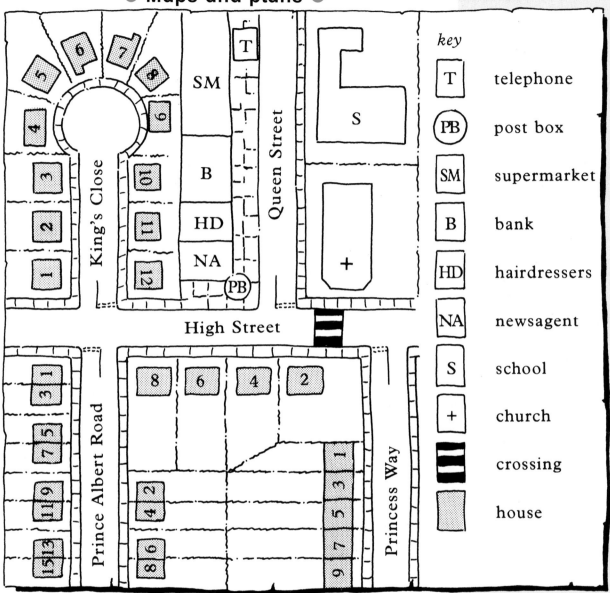

Answer these questions in your book.

1 What do these symbols mean?
   a) T   **b)** S   **c)** NA   **d)** +

2 How many houses are there in King's Close?

3 Where is the safest place to cross the High Street?

4 Where is the post-box? Describe its location. Now, write some directions to tell someone how to get from 9, Princess Way to the school.

WORD STUDY

● Words ending in 'tion' and 'sion' ●

Read the definitions of the unfinished words. Then, complete the words and write them in your book.

Use a dictionary to check your spellings.

1 where a train stops

s _ _ t i o n

2 you ask this

q u _ _ _ t i o n

3 an inventor makes this

i n _ _ _ _ t i o n

4 what you get at school

e d _ _ _ _ t i o n

5 something you watch

t e l e _ _ _ s i o n

6 when something is divided

_ _ _ v i s i o n

7 when something is extended

e x _ _ _ _ s i o n

8 when something explodes

_ _ _ p l _ _ s i o n

● Sort them out ●

*Choose either '**sion**' or '**tion**' to finish these words. Write the completed words in your book.*

1 crea _ _ _ _   2 pen _ _ _ _

3 vi _ _ _ _   4 na _ _ _ _

5 ac _ _ _ _   6 confu _ _ _ _

7 posi _ _ _ _   8 inva _ _ _ _

LANGUAGE STUDY

● Similes ●

*There are lots of **similes** in this poem. Copy it out in your best handwriting.*

As fierce as a tiger, as mild as a dove;

As stiff as a poker, as limp as a glove;

As blind as a bat, as deaf as a post;

As cool as a cucumber, as warm as toast;

As flat as a flounder, as round as a ball;

As blunt as a hammer, as sharp as an awl.

Anon

> A **simile** says what something is like, e.g. **as fierce as a tiger**.

*Give these **similes** suitable endings. Write them in your book.*

1 As wise as _____
2 As silly as _____
3 As quiet as _____
4 As noisy as _____
5 As straight as _____
6 As crooked as _____
7 As fat as _____
8 As thin as _____
9 As old as _____
10 As young as _____

> **extra**
> In the poem on page 22, there are several **similes**. Can you find them?

● Antonyms ●

*Think of sensible **antonyms** for these **verbs**. Write them in your book.*

1 **a)** push   **b)** move   **c)** throw   **d)** hate   **e)** buy

*Now, think of sensible **antonyms** for these **nouns**.*

2 **a)** enemy **b)** coward **c)** entrance **d)** boy   **e)** man

*Write down sensible **antonyms** for these **adjectives**.*

3 **a)** weak   **b)** tame   **c)** certain   **d)** guilty   **e)** crooked

*Finally, think of sensible **antonyms** for these **adverbs**.*

4 **a)** slowly **b)** noisily **c)** roughly **d)** messily **e)** sadly

> An **antonym** is a word that means the **opposite** of something, e.g. **hot** is the **antonym** of **cold**.

WRITING WORKSHOP

● Contractions ●

Match the long and short ways of saying the same thing. Write them in your book, like this:

What's the matter?   What is the matter?

What's the matter?	I am going out.
You can't do that!	It is not fair.
I'm going out.	I will soon be there.
You're wrong.	What is the matter?
It's not fair.	Let us go.
Don't do that.	You cannot do that!
Let's go.	You are wrong.
I'll soon be there.	Do not do that.

Apostrophes (') show where letters have been missed out of words. '**Don't** do that!' really means '**Do not** do that!'.

don't = do not

extra

*Think of some more 'shortened words' (**contractions**). Write them in your book.*

● Describing people ●

Read this description.

Mr Jones lives at Number 2. He's old and has a walking stick. He has very kind eyes. They twinkle when he smiles. Mr Jones has shaky hands. He's always cheerful, even though you can tell he hasn't got much money. He wears worn-out shoes. All my friends call him Jonah. He loves to hear us playing, and never minds when we make a noise on our bikes. He's a very nice man.

In your book, write a description of someone you know very well. Remember to write about:

- what they look like
- the way in which they speak, and the types of things they say
- their character (the sort of person they are)
- their habits or hobbies.

When you are writing a story, it is important to tell your readers as much as you can about the characters in it.

● Flying ●

- *Read the poem on page 22 again.*

- *Imagine you could fly with the boy. What would you smell, feel, hear and think while you were flying?*

- *Write your ideas in a chart in your book, like this:*

If I could fly I would:

smell	feel	hear	think
bacon cooking	the wind in my face	the whoosh of the wind	What if I get tired and fall?

> When you are writing, it is important to tell your readers about what you or your characters are thinking and feeling.

Turn some of your thoughts into a poem, like this:
    I can feel the gentle wind tugging at me.
    I feel great as I float and soar...

● Up, up and away! ●

If you could fly, where would you go:

to a far-off island?

to Disney World?

to New York?

Write a story about flying somewhere, and the adventures you have when you get there.

The lion with no courage

Dorothy: Come here, Toto, and stop barking. What have you found now?

Scarecrow: Oh! It's an enormous lion. I really can't fight him because I'm made of straw. He's pushing me over...

Tin Man: I will fight him. A lion cannot hurt me because I'm made of tin. I will hit him with my axe.

Dorothy: Take that, you horrible lion, and don't you dare bite my little dog. You ought to be ashamed of yourself, a big beast like you, biting my poor little dog.

Lion: I didn't bite him.

Dorothy: No, but you tried to. You are nothing but a great big coward.

Lion: I know that I am a great big coward. I have always known it, and I am very ashamed of myself.

Scarecrow: But that isn't right. The 'King of Beasts' shouldn't be a coward.

Lion: I know I shouldn't, but I was just born that way. All the other animals in the forest expect me to be brave, but the trouble is, I'm just scared of everything I see, even your little dog. Oh dear, I'm so unhappy.

Tin Man: He's crying. The Lion is crying. He's wiping his tears away with the tip of his tail. Here, keep away from me, or your tears will make me rusty again.

extra

Read 'The Wizard of Oz' to find out what happens to the characters.

Write the answers to these questions in your book.

COMPREHENSION

● Starting points ●

1 What was the dog's name?

2 What did the dog find?

3 What was the Tin Man going to hit the Lion with?

4 How did the Lion describe himself?

5 Why was the Tin Man afraid of the Lion's tears?

● Moving on ●

1 Where do you think Toto found the Lion?

2 What do the words below mean? Look them up in a dictionary if you are not sure.

   a) coward   **b)** ashamed   **c)** rusty

3 Write how you would help the lion if you were Dorothy.

STUDY SKILLS

● Looking for clues ●

Decide which pet belongs to each person. Write your answers in your book, and explain why you think they are correct.

I live on the top floor of a tall block of flats, so I don't go out much.

Mr Brown

I have a pond in my garden.

Sam

Their pets

I live in a small flat. There is no garden for me to play in.

I live on my own. I enjoy going out for walks.

Ben

Mr Stewart

I live on a farm in the country. There are lots of fields around the farm.

I live on my own, and have a pet for company. I can't walk very far any more.

Sarah

Mrs Church

WORD STUDY

● Prefixes - 'a', 'be' and 'de' ●

*In your book, write the **prefix 'a'**, **'be'** or **'de'** in front of each word, to form new words.*

1 [ ] came   2 [ ] part

3 [ ] lay   4 [ ] sleep

5 [ ] long   6 [ ] low

7 [ ] hind   8 [ ] cause

9 [ ] cross   10 [ ] serve

11 [ ] crease   12 [ ] gain

I've got no brains. I need your help!

● Words ending in 'able' and 'ible' ●

possible	comfortable	reliable

terrible   horrible

valuable   sensible   suitable

invisible   remarkable

Prefixes are letters that can be added to the beginning of words. **'Pre'** means **'before'**.

extra

Make up sentences using some of the words from the box.

Draw a chart like this in your book. Write the words from the box in the correct columns.

'- able'	'- ible'
valuable	

extra

Add two more words to each column.

30

LANGUAGE STUDY

● Proper nouns ●

I'm *Toto*.

My name is *Dorothy*.
I come from *Kansas*.

Wales	Nike	sheep	Ford	Mr Riaz
Divali	house	George Street	McDonalds	table
school	John Lennon	Sunday	Kent	Ms Smith

*Copy this chart into your book. Write the **proper nouns** from the box above in the correct columns.*

Person	Place	Brand name	Day/month/ special occasion
Mr Riaz	Wales		

*There are some words left-over. These are **common nouns**.*

● Collective nouns ●

a pride of lions

a bunch of flowers

*Complete each **collective noun** with a word from the box. Write the **nouns** in your book.*

1 A pack of _____ .

2 A fleet of _____ .

3 A library of _____ .

4 A forest of _____ .

5 A swarm of _____ .

6 A herd of _____ .

books

cards

trees

bees

cattle

ships

> **ℹ** A **proper noun** can be the name of a **person, place, brand, day, month or special occasion**. All proper nouns begin with **capital letters**.

> **ℹ** A **collective noun** is the name for a group of things e.g. a **bunch** of flowers.

> **extra**
>
> *Make up your own **collective nouns** for the following groups of things: bullies, clocks, jellies, motor bikes, dinosaurs, teachers. Write them in your book like this:*
> *a bother of bullies.*

31

WRITING WORKSHOP

● Speech marks ●

> When we write what people say in stories, we use **speech marks**. Whatever you would put in a speech bubble should be written between two sets of **speech marks**.

Copy and complete these sentences in your book.

"What big eyes you've got," Red Riding Hood said.

"_____ ," replied the Wolf.

"What sharp teeth you've got," _____ .

"_____ !" _____ .

> Whenever someone different speaks, start a new line.

Complete these sentences in your book.

Dorothy said, "_____ ."

"_____ ," replied the Tin Man.

Now, write out what the Scarecrow and Lion said in the same way.

extra

In your book, write out the play on page 28, with **speech marks** *in the correct places.*

● How do people see you? ●

*In the box are the names of people who said things about Beth.
In your book, write who you think said each thing.*

her older sister	her mum	her teacher
her best friend		her younger brother

> Beth is great. She'll never let you down. She knows how to keep a secret.

> Beth's a real chatterbox, but her reading is getting better.

> She's still a big baby. She's always sucking her thumb and cuddling her teddy.

> She always spoils my fun, and tells Mum when it's my bedtime.

> Beth is very helpful at home. She always keeps her bedroom tidy.

Beth

● Describing animals ●

Read this description of a pet cat. Notice how the author describes what the cat looks like and enjoys doing. In your book, write a description of a pet or an animal you know well.

His back, and his sides, and his legs as far as his socks would have come to, and his face and his ears and his tail were all marmalade coloured. His stomach and his waistcoat and his paws were white. And he had a white tassel at the tip of his tail, white fringes to his ears, and white whiskers. Most cats hate water, but Mog didn't. He loved it. He liked to sit by the tap, hitting the raindrops with his paw as they fell, and getting water all over his whiskers! The water made his marmalade fur go almost fox colour and his paws and waistcoat shining-white clean.

Joan Aitken

extra

Now write how four different people might describe you.

33

Do you remember? Test 1

STUDY SKILLS

For each set of words, choose the two words that are connected with the first one. Write the answers in your book like this:
      chair saucer <u>arm</u> face <u>leg</u> lid

1   flower   hands   purse   stem   petal   light

2   bicycle   wheel   pedal   cup   book   drawer

Write out these words in alphabetical order.

3   complaint   connect   coffee   course   collect

4   discuss   disguise   display   disaster   disease

Write the meanings of the underlined words in your book.

5   The game was <u>postponed</u> until the next week because of
    the snow.
      a) held   **b**) cancelled   **c**) put off

6   The rather <u>rotund</u> man enjoyed eating.
      a) tired   **b**) tall   **c**) fat

WORD STUDY

Copy these words into your book. Write if each one has 2, 3 or 4 syllables. The first one has been done for you.

1   difficult (3)   2 taken   3 manufacture

4   carefully   5 information   6 robot

Match the beginnings of the words to the correct endings. Write the completed words in your book.

7

penc	al
pan	el
fin	le
app	il

8

he	sion
hi	dge
sta	tch
vi	tion

34

LANGUAGE STUDY

*Copy these sentences into your book. Write if each of the underlined **verbs** is in the **present, past** or **future tense.***

1 Tomorrow, <u>it will</u> rain.

2 Last week, it <u>rained</u> a lot.

3 Today, it <u>is raining</u>.

*Copy and complete these **similes** with suitable words.*

4 as smooth as _____   5 as tall as _____

6 as _____ as a mouse   7 as _____ as an owl

*Think of suitable **collective nouns** to go in the spaces. Write them in your book.*

8 a _____ of flowers   9 a _____ of sheep

10 a _____ of wolves   11 a _____ of bees

WRITING WORKSHOP

*Copy these sentences into your book. Add **speech marks** in the correct places.*

1 How old are you? he asked.

2 The salesman said, This car is very fast.

3 You're early, the teacher said.

4 Get the ball, he shouted.

Copy out this passage and punctuate it correctly.

it was a warm light summer
evening greg the giant was sitting
at home feeling rather lonely suddenly
there was a loud knock at the
door when greg opened the door
he was surprised to see his friend
george there what a lovely surprise
greg said lets go and see if we can
find someone to annoy george
said greg thought this was a
great idea they both went off
happily looking for trouble

35

Cat's eyes

Percy Shaw was born in 1890. He was the son of a factory worker, and one of fourteen children. When Percy grew up, he got a job repairing roads.

One night, Percy was driving home through a thick fog. It was extremely tiring and frightening trying to drive in such conditions.

Suddenly, Percy saw two bright spots of light appear in front of the car. Then they were gone. In a flash, he realised what they were - cat's eyes! He hadn't been able to see the rest of the cat, but its eyes had reflected the light coming from the car headlights.

Percy thought a great deal about what happened that evening. An idea began to form in his head. In the next few months, he spent hours experimenting in his workshop. One day, he shouted with excitement - his idea worked. He had designed some round, glass studs that reflected the light from a car's headlights as the car came towards them. If a row of these studs was put down the centre of a road, car drivers would see them and be able to drive safely - even in the worst fogs. By the time he died, in 1976, Percy's invention was in use throughout Britain and the rest of the world.

Think of sensible words to go in the spaces. Write them in your book.

COMPREHENSION

● Starting points ●

Percy was born in __1__ . His job was to __2__ roads. One night, it was very __3__ when Percy was driving home. He saw two __4__ of light appear in the road ahead. They were __5__ eyes that had __6__ the light from his car's headlights. This gave Percy an __7__ . He designed some round, __8__ studs. When these 'cat's eyes' are placed in the __9__ of the road, they __10__ cars at night.

● Moving on ●

Now, answer these questions in your book.

1 What do these words mean?
   a) reflected   **b**) designed   **c**) prevented

2 Why are roads so dangerous? List some reasons.

3 What inventions help to make roads safer? List some of them.

Look up the words in a dictionary if you are not sure.

STUDY SKILLS

● Using charts and grids ●

Name	Born	Place of birth	Famous for:	Died
Baird, John Logie	1888	Helensborough, Scotland	inventing television in 1923	1946
Brunel, Isambard Kingdom	1806	Portsmouth, England	designing first steamship in 1838	1859
Fleming, Alexander	1881	Ayrshire, Scotland	discovering penicillin in 1928	1955
Gutenberg, Johann	1398	Mainz, Germany	inventing first printing machine around 1440	1468
Issigonis, Alec	1906	Izmir, Turkey	designing the mini car in 1956	1988
Newton, Isaac	1642	Woolsthorpe, England	discovering gravity around 1665	1727

This is a table of information about famous scientists and inventors. Use the information to answer these questions in your book.

1 Who was born the longest time ago?

2 Who died most recently?

3 Which two men were born in Scotland?

4 Who invented television?

5 Who discovered penicillin?

Write out the names of the scientists and inventors in the order in which they were born - starting with the oldest.

extra

Use an encyclopedia to find out more about one of these people. Copy some interesting facts into your book.

WORD STUDY

● Matching words and meanings ●

*In your book, write each '**wor**' word next to its meaning.*

- a wiggly creature
- something you say
- the planet on which we live
- value
- a job
- opposite of best

word
worst
work
worm
worth
world

> **i** '**w**' + '**or**' is pronounced '**wer**', e.g. **wor**ld and **wor**d.

> **extra**
> *Make up sentences using some of the '**wor**' words.*

*Now match these '**wa**' words with their meanings.*

- a flying insect
- something a wizard waves
- to walk slowly
- boggy ground
- this measures the time
- to clean yourself
- to gulp
- a white bird with a long neck

wander
wash
swamp
wand
wasp
watch
swan
swallow

> **i** '**w**' + '**a**' is pronounced '**wo**', e.g. **wa**sp and **wa**sh.

> **extra**
> *Make up some sentences with '**wa**' words in them.*

38

LANGUAGE STUDY

● Verb tenses - past, present and future ●

Copy and complete this chart.

Past tense (yesterday)	Present tense (now)	Future tense (tomorrow)
I jumped.	I jump.	I will jump.
I shouted.	I shout.	
	I kick.	I will kick.
I dived.		
	I run.	
		I will fall.
I swam.		

*Rewrite the passage below in your book. All the **verbs** should be written in the **past tense**. Do it like this:*

Tod <u>liked</u> his dog.

Tod <u>likes</u> his dog. He <u>strokes</u> him and <u>feeds</u> him. He <u>takes</u> him for walks and <u>gives</u> him lots of love.

*Now, rewrite this passage in your book. All the **verbs** should be written in the **future tense**. Do it like this:*

Marie will <u>stay</u> at her friend's house on Saturday.

Marie <u>stayed</u> at her friend's house on Saturday. She <u>listened</u> to music and <u>watched</u> TV. The two girls <u>went</u> to bed late. Marie's dad <u>collected</u> her on Sunday morning.

> **ℹ** The way we write verbs changes, depending on whether things happen in the **past**, **present** or **future**.

extra

*In your book, write the **past tenses** of these verbs:*

talk - <u>talked</u>
bake - _____
look - _____
tap - _____
rub - _____
open - _____

*Now, write the **past tenses** of these verbs - but be careful!*

speak - _____
find - _____
hold - _____
break - _____
go - _____
buy - _____

WRITING WORKSHOP

● Apostrophes: possession ●

Look at the pairs of pictures. In your book, complete the pairs of sentences like this:

The banana <u>belongs to</u> the monkey.
It is the <u>monkey's banana</u>.

monkey   banana

> **ℹ** **Apostrophes** (') are used to show **possession** - that a thing **belongs to** someone or something. If something **belongs** to one person/thing, we add **'s** to the end of their name, like this:
>
> The dog**'s** bone.

The tail _____ the lion.
It is the _____ .

The stethoscope _____ the doctor.
It is the _____ .

The snorkel _____ the swimmer.
It is the _____ .

> **extra**
>
> *Mix up some of the pairs of pictures, and make up silly sentences to go with them, e.g.: The knitting belongs to the doctor. It is the doctor's knitting.*

The knitting _____ Granny.
It is _____ .

*Draw these signs in your book. Add **apostrophes** in the correct places.*

BOBS BAKERY

HARRIETS HAIRDRESSING SALON

WEBSTERS SUPERMARKET

PIETROS PIZZA

Janes Antique Shop

ALIS CARPETS

● Making rules ●

Write down as many road safety rules as you can think of:
- *Choose the five most important ones.*
- *Include them in a 'road safety' notice, like this:*

 Your notice should have:

- a catchy, clear title
- a well-drawn, bold but simple picture
- your five rules on it, written out neatly
- your notice should take up a whole page.

● Writing instructions ●

Rewrite the instructions for using this bottle of shampoo. They are in the wrong order.

- Rub the shampoo into the hair until it lathers.
- Towel or blow-dry your shining, clean hair.
- First dampen your hair with warm water.
- Wash the hair until it is thoroughly clean.
- Rinse off the lather.
- Then, apply a small amount of shampoo.
- Apply some more shampoo.

Write some instructions for how to do one of these things:

a) make a cup of tea

b) make a simple cardboard mask

c) put a new battery into a toy

d) mow the lawn

extra

Write out the rules for playing one of these games:

- *Noughts and Crosses*
- *Conkers*
- *Marbles*
- *Snap.*

Remember to explain:

- *what you need, e.g. a piece of paper for Noughts and Crosses*

- *how to play the game.*

41

The stinger

Luton/Bedfordshire on Sunday, August 27th 1995

New police weapon takes the joy out of vehicle theft

Non-lethal weapon: Sergeant Alan Bell with the Stinger

TRAFFIC POLICE in Bedfordshire have a 'sting in the tail' for joy-riders and drunk drivers. The Stinger is an American invention that will stop a speeding car dead within twenty seconds. This reusable device is to be kept in police vehicles and placed across the road when required.

The Stinger has hollow spikes that penetrate a suspect vehicle's tyres, slowly letting the air out and stopping the vehicle. This device is said to be completely safe, as it brings vehicles to a gradual halt without a loss of control. Road Traffic Officer, Alan Bell, believes the device will prevent the need for dangerous high-speed pursuits.

At present, Bedfordshire has only five Stingers but more are on order. 'In the very near future, every traffic car will have them,' said Sergeant Bell.

COMPREHENSION

● Starting points ●

1 In which country was the Stinger invented?

2 What is the Stinger used for?

3 Why is the Stinger said to be very safe?

4 What is the name of the police officer mentioned in the report?

● Moving on ●

Now, answer these questions.

1 Why is it better to use the Stinger than have police chasing car thieves?

2 What do these words mean? (You can look them up in a dictionary.) **a**) penetrate **b**) gradual

3 Why do you think people steal cars? List some reasons.

Write the answers to these questions in your book.

42

STUDY SKILLS

● Points of view ●

In your book, write what these people might say about the Stinger:

a) a policeman
b) a car thief

Now, write what these people might say about school:

a) a teacher **b**) a parent **c**) a child

● Fact and opinion ●

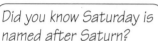

Copy these sentences into your book. Write whether each one is a ***fact*** *or an* ***opinion***.

1 I think Manchester United are great!

2 St Paul's Cathedral is in London.

3 Rome is the capital city of Italy.

4 Chewing gum is better than chocolate.

5 Cars are a nuisance. Bikes are best.

6 Some cars are made in Germany.

In your ***opinion***, *what is the best:*

● sweet   ● pop group   ● TV programme?

In your book, write one ***fact*** *about your favourite:*

● sweet   ● pop group   ● TV programme.

> ⓘ A **fact** is something that can usually be proved. An **opinion** is what someone thinks, and may or may not be true.

WORD STUDY

● What a difference a 'p' makes! ●

Copy these word endings into your book. Write either 're' or 'pre' in front of them, so that they make sense.

1	☐	use	**2**	☐	dict	**3**	☐	tend
4	☐	fill	**5**	☐	pare	**6**	☐	call
7	☐	fect	**8**	☐	vent	**9**	☐	place
10	☐	mind	**11**	☐	turn	**12**	☐	fix

extra

Think of some other words that begin with 're' or 'pre'. Write them in your book.

● Looking for 'gu' and 'qu' words ●

Read this poster. Find all the words that contain 'gu'. List them in your book. Then, make a separate list of all the 'qu' words.

CARL'S CLASSIC CARS

No need:
- to quiver or quake - you can trust us!
- to guard against rogues - you can rely on us!
- to quibble over price - we've got the lowest prices in town.
- for vague promises - we guarantee every car.

If you require credit, enquire about our special terms. For quick, reliable service come to:

CARL'S CLASSIC CARS

1 We often put a 'u' after a 'g' if it is followed by an 'e' or an 'i': **gu**ess, **gu**itar.

2 The letter 'u' always follows 'q'. Together, these letters make a 'kw' sound: **qu**iet, **qu**een.

44

LANGUAGE STUDY

Adjectives
● - making sentences more interesting ●

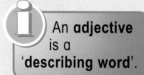

An **adjective** is a 'describing word'.

*Rewrite these sentences without the **adjectives**.*

1 The scruffy thief stole the shiny, new car.

2 The old man sat down on the wooden bench.

3 The small girl climbed the tall, oak tree.

4 The huge, hairy monster leapt out of the dark cave.

*Copy these sentences into your book. Make them more interesting by adding **adjectives**.*

1 The giant marched into the castle.

2 A dragon guarded the treasure.

3 The girl ate a cake.

4 The boy ran away from the creature.

extra

Imagine that you have just seen a car being stolen. Write a good description of the thief for the police.

*Do it like this and underline all the **adjectives**:*

Jake has a <u>long</u> beard. He has <u>short</u>, <u>black</u> hair and a <u>jagged</u> scar down his <u>left</u> cheek.

● Comparing adjectives ●

strong   stronger   strongest

Copy and complete this chart.

Adjective	Comparative form of adjective	Superlative form of adjective
heavy	heavier	heaviest
hairy		hairiest
noisy		
	lazier	laziest
busy		
	uglier	
		tidiest

extra

*Choose one **adjective** from the chart. Draw cartoon pictures to show the differences between the three forms of it.*

WRITING WORKSHOP

● Correct the punctuation ●

Rewrite this newspaper article in your book. It needs to be punctuated correctly.

CAR THIEF ARRESTED

last night the police gave chase to a stolen ford car the car had been taken from a car park in luton and was being driven towards london after a long dangerous chase the stolen car was stopped james newton said i cant stop im in a hurry this is my mothers car ive just borrowed it the police arrested mr newton who spent last night in jail hell appear in court on monday

● Writing a report from notes ●

You are a reporter. You have just been talking to some people who were rescued from a sinking ship. Here are some notes you took.

> S.O.S. call - ship in distress
>
> storm - rocks - helicopter
>
> rescue - survivors - medal

Use the notes to write a report for your newspaper. You will need to:
- *give it a catchy headline*
- *draw a picture to go with it*
- *write a caption (label) under the picture.*

extra

Choose one of these headlines as the title for a story:
- *DISASTER AT SCHOOL!*
- *GIANT RAT ESCAPES!*
- *TEACHER STRIKES IT RICH!*

46

● Reporting ●

extra

Write one thing each of these people might say about the accident:

- *Mr Bun the Baker*
- *the policeman*
- *a local road safety officer*
- *the van driver's boss.*

Mrs Simmons saw the accident.
This is how she described it
to the policeman.

I was just walking along the High Street, when suddenly I heard the screeching of brakes. When I looked round, I saw the van skidding across the road. I saw a cat running away. Maybe the driver swerved to avoid the cat, I don't know. He may have been going too fast. Cars do speed along this road.

Imagine that you are the driver.
In your book, write what you would say to the policemen.

● Speech marks ●

*Copy these sentences into your book. Add **speech marks** in the correct places. The first one has been done for you.*

1 I'm going to school Tom said.
   "I'm going to school," Tom said.

2 It's raining said Beth.

3 I've lost my book Mark said.

4 Wait for me! shouted Shiva.

5 What do you think you're doing? the policeman asked.

6 I'm hungry moaned Shagufta.

47

Dear Mr Merlin

Dear Mr Merlin

Could you fix it for me
to be a wizard for the day?
Please send me an invitation
- I'd love to come and stay.

I'd get all the proper gear,
black cloak and pointed hat,
sprinkle them with star shapes
and bring my own pet bat.

If I can be your assistant
I'll work hard all day long.
I'll stir the simmering cauldron
till the spells are hot and strong.

I'll gladly add in eyes of newts
and spiders by the load,
If you can fix a recipe to
turn my brother into a toad.

You're a modern man, Mr Merlin,
I know you couldn't care less
that I'm not some ambitious boy
but an apprentice wizardress.

Love from

Lucy
x x x

Moira Andrews

*Choose the right answers
and write them in your book.*

COMPREHENSION

● Starting points ●

1 Who wrote the letter?
   a) Lucky   **b**) Lenny   **c**) Lucy

2 Who was the letter addressed to?
   a) Mr Merlin   **b**) Mr Magician   **c**) Mr Merton

3 What did Lucy say she would wear?
   a) a red cloak   **b**) a purple cloak   **c**) a black cloak

4 What did Lucy want to turn her brother into?
   a) a toad   **b**) a frog   **c**) a spider

5 What pet did Lucy say she would bring along?
   a) a frog   **b**) a bat   **c**) a newt

6 What animals' eyes did Lucy say she would put in the
   cauldron?
   a) spiders and newts   **b**) snakes and snails
   c) bats and cats

● Moving on ●

Now, answer these questions in your book.

1 Who do you think Mr Merlin is? Explain your answer.

2 Where do you think he might live? List some places.

3 What do these words mean? (If you are not sure, look them up in a dictionary.)
    a) assistant   **b)** simmering

4 Did you like the poem? Explain your answer.

STUDY SKILLS

● Using a glossary ●

> A glossary is like a small dictionary, at the back of a book, which tells you what difficult words in the book mean.

Glossary _____

ambitious - wanting to do well

apprentice - a person who is taught a trade by a skilled worker

cauldron - a large, heavy, iron cooking pot

plague - *a)* a fatal epidemic or infestation of pests *b)* to pester or annoy

reptile - a cold-blooded creature that has a backbone and moves by creeping or crawling

scale - *a)* one of the many flat plates that cover certain animals, especially reptiles and fish *b)* an instrument used for weighing *c)* to climb up

---

> Here is part of the **glossary** from a book about wizards.

*Use the **glossary** to answer these questions in your book.*

1 Which words have more than one meaning? List them.

2 How would you describe someone who wants to do well?

3 What is the name of a large cooking pot used by wizards?

4 Are reptiles hot or cold-blooded?

WORD STUDY

● Words ending in 'our' or 'ous' ●

Find the five **'our'** *and five* **'ous'** *words in the cauldron.*
Write them in your book.

a	f	l	a	v	o	u	r	b	c
d	e	f	g	f	a	m	o	u	s
j	e	a	l	o	u	s	h	i	j
k	l	m	h	a	r	b	o	u	r
n	c	o	l	o	u	r	p	q	s
d	a	n	g	e	r	o	u	s	t
u	v	e	n	o	r	m	o	u	s
r	u	m	o	u	r	w	x	y	z
b	e	h	a	v	i	o	u	r	q
b	c	n	e	r	v	o	u	s	d

Look into my cauldron and you will see some **'our'** *and* **'ous'** *words hiding from you and me!*

Use the **'our'** *and* **'ous'** *from the cauldron to complete these sentences in your book.*

1 Red is a _____ .

2 The pop star was very _____ .

3 I heard a _____ that you had won the lottery.

4 The apple pie had a lovely _____ .

5 The busy road was very _____ .

6 The ship came into the _____ .

7 The wizard's _____ was very strange.

8 I was _____ of my friend's new trainers.

9 I was very _____ when I entered the creepy, old house.

10 I ate an _____ dinner.

extra

Look at these **'ous'** *words carefully. When you think you can remember them, cover them up and try to write them in your book without copying.*

poisonous
adventurous
mysterious
fabulous
luxurious

LANGUAGE STUDY

● Gender - masculine and feminine ●

Match the **masculine** and **feminine** forms of these nouns.
List the pairs of words in your book like this:

king   queen

masculine	prince king father lord
	lion bull drake stallion

feminine	queen lioness mare mother
	princess duck cow lady

> **i** Masculine means **male** and **feminine** means **female**: 'boy' is **masculine** and 'girl' is **feminine**.

● Adverbs ●

Read these sentences. Write them in your book, replacing the underlined words with the correct **adverbs** from the box.

1 The dog barked <u>with a loud noise</u>.

2 The dog snarled <u>in an angry way</u>.

3 The dog ran <u>at a great speed</u>.

4 The dog chased the stick <u>with enthusiasm</u>.

5 The dog wagged its tail <u>in a happy manner</u>.

> **i** Adverbs tell us more about **verbs**. They often end in 'ly'.

angrily

happily

enthusiastically

loudly

quickly

Copy the chart below into your book. Change the **adjectives** in the box into **adverbs** ending in '**ly**'. Write them in the correct columns of your chart. The first few have been done for you.

brave   lucky   gentle   hopeful   skilful
comfortable   heavy   easy   simple   horrible   sudden
equal   possible   clumsy   plain   angry

Just add 'ly'	Change the 'y' to 'i' and add 'ly'	Drop the 'e' and add 'ly'
bravely	*luckily*	*gently*

> **extra**
> *Choose two **adverbs** from each column. Write some sentences using them.*

51

WRITING WORKSHOP

● Writing letters ●

Read the poem on page 48 again. Here is the letter that Mr Merlin wrote back to Lucy.

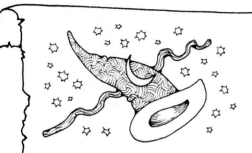

10 Abracadabra Gardens
Zim Zallabim
Hocus Pocushire
HP17 RX4

October 25th 2001

Dear Lucy,

　　Thank you for your letter. I am delighted to hear that you want to be a wizardress, although I'm not sure it's a good idea to turn your brother into a toad!

　　I do run training programmes for anyone who wishes to become a wizard or a wizardress. Unfortunately I do not run day courses, so you would have to come and stay for a while. Not everyone is cut out to be a wizard or wizardress, so I am very careful who I train. Perhaps you would be kind enough to write to me again, telling me something about yourself. Please feel free to ask questions about the training programmes.

　　Yours sincerely,

Pretend that you are Lucy, and write a letter back to Mr Merlin:

- Tell him some interesting things about yourself - the sort of person you are, your hobbies etc.

- Say why you think you would make a good wizard or wizardress.

- Remember to ask some questions about the training programmes. You could ask how long they would last or how much they would cost.

---

i All letters should have the following features:

- the address and postcode in the top right-hand corner
- the date underneath
- the name of the person you're writing to on the left
- a new line for a new idea.
- The name of the person who wrote the letter at the bottom. (Just before this should be written 'Love', if you're writing to someone you know well, or 'Yours sincerely' if you don't know them well.)

extra

Draw an envelope in your book and address it to Mr Merlin.

52

● Spells ●

Read this spell from Macbeth, written by William Shakespeare.

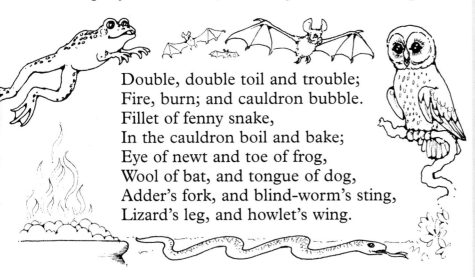

Double, double toil and trouble;
Fire, burn; and cauldron bubble.
Fillet of fenny snake,
In the cauldron boil and bake;
Eye of newt and toe of frog,
Wool of bat, and tongue of dog,
Adder's fork, and blind-worm's sting,
Lizard's leg, and howlet's wing.

extra

See what you can find out about:
- William Shakespeare
- the story of the 'Sorcerer's Apprentice'.

In your book, write a spell of your own. Before you start, decide what you want your spell to do - it could turn water into lemonade or your friend into a toad. Then:

- In rough, write a list of the ingredients for your spell.
- Experiment with your list. Add **adjectives**, **verbs** and **sound words**.
- Choose the best ideas and copy out the spell in your best handwriting.
- Draw a picture underneath your spell.

extra

Imagine you find a spell book but something goes badly wrong. Write a story about your troubles.

● Recipes ●

Read this recipe for happiness.

Take a ray of sunshine,
A fluffy cloud,
The whisper of evening,
The lapping of the sea,
A handful of golden sand,
Some everlasting sweets.
Stir them together
And let me dream!

Now, write your own recipe for happiness.

THE INNUIT, who many people call the Eskimos, believe that a long time ago the Earth dropped out of the skies. Many babies appeared on the Earth and were found by a man and a woman. The woman made clothes for the babies. The man stamped his foot on the ground, and suddenly dogs appeared. They helped him hunt for food. Ever since, dogs have been important to the Innuit.

At first the Earth was dark, since there was no light in the world, and people were immortal. One day two women had an argument about this. The first woman said that as long as it was dark they could not get older, and therefore would not die. The second woman said that she would rather begin to die than live in darkness all the time. She won the argument, and light appeared on the Earth, which is why people now grow old and die.

Another Innuit story says that one day a brother and a sister had a quarrel. They both lit torches in the darkness, and the woman ran away into the sky. Her brother chased after her, but, as he ran, his torch began to go out. The woman's torch grew brighter and brighter, and she became the Sun. Her brother became the Moon. *Jon Mayled*

COMPREHENSION

● Starting points ●

1 Another name for the Eskimos is...

2 The woman made...

3 When the man stamped his foot...

4 When the Earth was in darkness...

5 After the quarrel, the brother became...

Copy these beginnings of sentences into your book. Give them sensible endings.

● Moving on ●

Answer these questions in your book.

1 Stories about how the Earth might have been formed are sometimes called 'creation myths'. What do you think a 'myth' is?

2 Which two words in the passage mean to 'have a row'?

3 What do you think are the advantages and disadvantages of being 'immortal' (living for ever)? Make two lists.

STUDY SKILLS

● Guide words ●

'Below' is the first word on page 11.

'Bit' is the last word on page 11.

below	*page 11*	bit

below under, lower down, beneath, less than.

belt *a)* a strip of leather, etc. used to fasten trousers around the waist

bicycle a two wheeled pedal vehicle.

bid *a)* an offer to buy something for a certain price. *b)* an attempt to do something. *c)* an old-fashioned

Bible The sacred book of the Jewish and Christian religions.

biceps the large muscles on the upper arms.

once common in North America, related to cattle.

bit *a)* a small piece *b)* the smallest unit of information in a computer's

Which three of these words would appear on page 11? List them in your book.

beneath   bin   beak   burn   blossom   bird

fold	*page 42*	fragile	fragrant	*page 43*	furious

Which of these words should go on page 42, and which should go on page 43? Write two separate lists in your book.

food   frown   funnel   fork   freeze   fraction

There are **guide words** on each page of a dictionary, which can help you to find words more easily.

extra

Think of three words that could fit between the **guide words**:

a) somewhere and special
b) chalk and chicken.

Here are some more dictionary pages. Look at the **guide words**.

WORD STUDY

● Words ending in 'ness' ●

Which of these words can you add 'ness' to? Write the words in your book like this: <u>darkness</u>

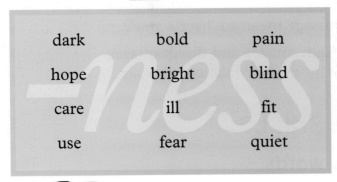

dark	bold	pain
hope	bright	blind
care	ill	fit
use	fear	quiet

Check your answers using a dictionary.

● Words beginning with 'in' or 'im' ●

*The wrong **prefix** has been put at the beginning of each of these words. Rewrite them correctly in your book.*

imcome	inportant
imdoors	inmortal
imform	inmediate
imdeed	inmense
imside	inagine
imtense	initate

---

extra

*Change these **adjectives** ending in '**y**' into **nouns** ending in '**ness**', like this: **lazy - laziness**. Write them in your book.*

- *heavy*
- *lonely*
- *happy*
- *busy*
- *noisy*
- *dirty*

---

extra

*Choose two '**in**' and two '**im**' words. Make up some sentences that include these words.*

LANGUAGE STUDY

● Singulars and plurals ●

Rule 1	Rule 2	Rule 3
For **nouns** ending in '**f**' or '**fe**', change the ending to '**ves**': knife - knives.	For **nouns** ending in a **consonant** + '**y**', drop the '**y**' and add '**ies**': baby - babies.	For **nouns** ending in a **consonant** + '**o**', you would usually add '**es**': potato - potatoes.

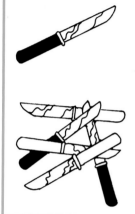 

> **Singular** means one of something, e.g. **a pen**. **Plural** means more than one of something, e.g. **lots of pens**.

*In your book write the **plurals** of these nouns:*

1 fly	2 hero	3 wolf	4 loaf	5 lady
6 volcano	7 family	8 leaf	9 Eskimo	10 echo
11 thief	12 cargo	13 factory	14 half	15 tomato

> Some **plurals** do not follow any rules, you just have to learn them!

*Match each **singular** noun to the correct **plural**. Write them in your book like this:*

   foot - feet

Singular nouns	Plurals
foot	gateaux sheep feet
child	mice deer teeth dice
man	geese children men
die	
mouse	
tooth	
gateau	
deer	
goose	
sheep	

> You say house and houses. Why can't you say mouse and mouses?

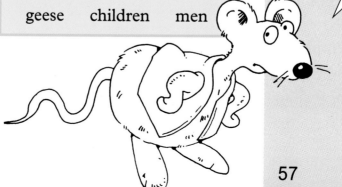

WRITING WORKSHOP

● Using conjunctions ●

Write these beginnings of sentences in your book. Add a suitable ending after each **conjunction.**

1 Accidents happen because...

2 Tom was glad when...

3 They arrived at the station where...

4 Beth was playing in the garden although...

5 We ran for shelter as...

6 I bought an ice cream from the man who...

● Making two sentences into one ●

Join these pairs of sentences and write them in your book. The first one has been done for you.

1 The dog was hungry. It wanted to go into the house for its dinner.
   The hungry dog wanted to go into the house for its dinner.

2 The lion was angry. It was caught in a trap.

3 The motorist was dizzy. He had been in an accident.

4 The man was lucky. He had just won the lottery.

5 The lorry was old. It could not travel very fast.

6 The cat was frightened. It ran away.

● Missing punctuation ●

Punctuate these sentences correctly in your book.

1 i dont like football

2 please get me some sweets a lolly an ice cream and a comic

3 the aeroplane flew in from america

4 crash the car hit a tree

5 wheres ben mrs brown asked

> **Conjunctions** are '**joining words**' - they can be used to join two sentences together. It was getting darker. I put on the light.
>
> When a conjunction is used this becomes:
> It was getting darker **so** I put on the light.

58

Writing stories -
● beginnings, middles and endings ●

Beginning

*Here is the **beginning** of a story.*

King Edwanda was absolutely fed up. When he woke up, it was dark. When he had lunch, it was dark. When he went for a walk, it was dark. It was always dark. How he wished for some light in the world. One day, he could stand it no more, so he summoned his son, Nahum, and his daughter, Mareka. The King set them a challenge. He ordered them to go in search of light. They were not to return until they found it.

Middle

*Write the **middle** of the story in your book. Here are some things that could happen to Nahum and Mareka while they are searching for light. They could:*

- go to a forest
- meet a wise owl
- meet the 'Dragon of Darkness'
- go to Mystery Mountain.

Ending

Make up an exciting or unusual ending for your story.

● Arguments ●

Answer these questions in your book.

- Do you ever argue at home?
- Who do you argue with?
- What do you argue about?
- How do you feel when you argue?
- What do you say? How do you act?

Write about an argument you have had.

extra

In your book, list some things:

- you can do to prevent arguments

- people do when they are angry.

59

Do you remember?

STUDY SKILLS

Write who you think said these things about the rain. Choose from the people listed in the box.

child

farmer

shopper

1 It's lovely. It's just what the crops need.

2 I hope I've got my umbrella with me.

3 It's horrible. It means I can't go out to play.

*Copy these statements. Write next to each one whether it is a **fact** or an **opinion**.*

4 Rain is wet.

5 I don't like rain. It's a nuisance.

6 Rain falls from the sky.

7 Rain is lovely to splash in.

8 *In your book, write three words that might be found in a dictionary between these **guide words**.*

hammer	hasty

WORD STUDY

In each row, choose the correct endings to make three sensible words. Write the answers in your book like this:

   1. word, work, worse.

1	wo ___	_ _ rd	_ _ f	_ _ lk	_ _ rk	_ _ rse
2	wa ___	_ _ np	_ _ sd	_ _ sp	_ _ sh	_ _ nt
3	re ____	_ _ mind	_ _ tend	_ _ turb	_ _ place	_ _ turn
4	pre ___	_ _ _ tend	_ _ _ use	_ _ _ pare	_ _ _ dict
5	gu ___	_ _ ard	_ _ iz	_ _ ess	_ _ een	_ _ ide
6	qu ___	_ _ ite	_ _ ick	_ _ irl	_ _ ood	_ _ estion

LANGUAGE STUDY

*Rewrite the **verbs** in this passage in the **future tense**.*

1 Beth <u>ran</u> home from school. She <u>ate</u> her tea quickly
and <u>went</u> to call for her friend. They <u>went</u> to the sports
centre. They <u>had</u> a great time there. They <u>swam</u> and
<u>played</u> on the slide.

*Copy these sentences into your book. Complete them with the
correct **comparative adjectives**.*

2 I am noisy, but John is _____ than me. Beth is
the _____ of us all.

3 My bag is heavy, but Mrs Smith's bag is much _____.
My dad's tool bag is the _____ bag I've ever lifted.

4 Blob was an ugly monster, but Blab was even _____.
Their friend, Blub, was the _____ monster on Earth.

*Change these **adjectives** into **adverbs** and write them in your
book. The first one has been done for you.*

5 quick - <u>*quickly*</u>   6 slow - _____

7 happy - _____   8 easy - _____

9 gentle - _____   10 quiet - _____

*Think of a word with an **apostrophe** to go in each space.
Write the words in your book like this: 11. cat's*

11 The ___<u>cat's</u>___ fur was black.

12 The _____ bone was in the bowl.

13 The _____ trunk is very bendy.

14 The _____ spines are very prickly.

15 The _____ poison is very deadly.

WRITING WORKSHOP

Copy this passage and punctuate it correctly.

ben was watching television the programme he was
watching hadnt finished come on its time for bed youll
never get up in time for school if you dont go now said his
mum its not fair im never allowed to see the end of my
programme ben shouted he stamped up the stairs in a mood

MANY creatures dwell in the rainforest. There are sloths, tapirs, ant-eaters and Blue Morpho butterflies. Toucans, macaws and monkeys live in the forest canopy. There is plenty of food and water for all the creatures, whether they make their home in the trees or on the ground. One day, the forest stirred. From afar, there came a terrible tale.

The birds had lost their perches. All the trees were falling down! Toucan heard this message with deep foreboding. Sloth was also worried. He felt rumblings in the forest.
A strange scent floated on the wind, causing the Blue Morpho butterflies to flutter higher among the treetops. The macaws, too, sensed something sinister in the air. The ant-eaters stopped foraging, and crept into the undergrowth. Tapirs trooped off into the shadows. Howler monkey screeched a warning to his fellows. They heard him miles away. Jaguar roared with fury, and sped through the trees. The animals shuddered. Jaguar was the most powerful creature in the rainforest.

But something even more powerful was threatening their world. Machines! Cutting and spoiling! Jaguar heard a voice.
'Go to high ground,' it said. 'Go to high ground.'

The rains came as the animals made their way higher and higher. Fear drove them on. Then the floods came! There were no trees to hold the soil in place, so the river burst its banks. The machines were washed away! But the creatures of the rainforest were safe. The animals looked down on the swirling water, the broken tree trunks, and the muddy banks, and wondered how long the tall trees would be there to guard them.

Helen Cowcher

COMPREHENSION

● Starting points ●

1 Where does the story take place?
    a) on a farm   **b**) in the woods   **c**) in the rainforest

2 Where do toucans live in the forest?
    a) in the river   **b**) in the canopy   **c**) in the undergrowth

3 What floated in on the wind?
    a) a strange scent   **b**) butterflies   **c**) strange sounds

4 Who roared in fury?
    a) a lion   **b**) a tiger   **c**) a jaguar

5 What was threatening the world of the rainforest?
    a) machines   **b**) floods   **c**) storms

6 Were the machines:
    a) stolen   **b**) washed away   **c**) broken?

Choose the correct answers. Write them in your book.

● Moving on ●

Now, answer these questions in your book.

1. What do these words mean? If you are not sure, look them up in a dictionary.
   a) dwell   **b**) foreboding   **c**) sinister

2. Read the second paragraph of the 'Rainforest' again. What do you feel as you read it?

3. This is a modern tale, with a message for the reader. What is the author trying to make you think about?

STUDY SKILLS

● Using an encyclopedia ●

This is an **encyclopedia** in seven volumes.

Information in **encyclopedias** is set out in **alphabetical order**.

1. *Study the picture. Write down in which volume you would look up:*

   a) ant-eaters   **b**) sloths   **c**) macaws
   d) jaguars   **e**) tapirs   **f**) parrots

Choose two of the animals mentioned in the story. Find out and write down some interesting facts about them.

2. *Copy this list of topics into your book. For each one, underline the word you would look up in the **encyclopedia** to find information about it. Also, write the volume you would look in. The first one has been done for you.*

   a) creatures of the <u>rainforest</u>   *volume 6*
   b) sailing a yacht   _____
   c) how a telescope works   _____
   d) parts of the body   _____
   e) The Himalayan Mountains   _____
   f) John Dunlop   _____

3. *Now, think of two other topics that you might find information about in each volume. List them in your book.*

63

WORD STUDY

● 'Root' words ●

*Copy these words into your book. Underline the smaller, '**root**' word in each one, like this:*

<u>shop</u>ping

shopping	wetter	cleaned	diver
excited	hopeful	lonesome	careless
lately	safety	patted	rainy

● Words ending in 'ure' ●

*Finish off these words by adding '**ure**', and copy them into your book. Write the correct meaning next to each word, like this:*

Injure means to harm.

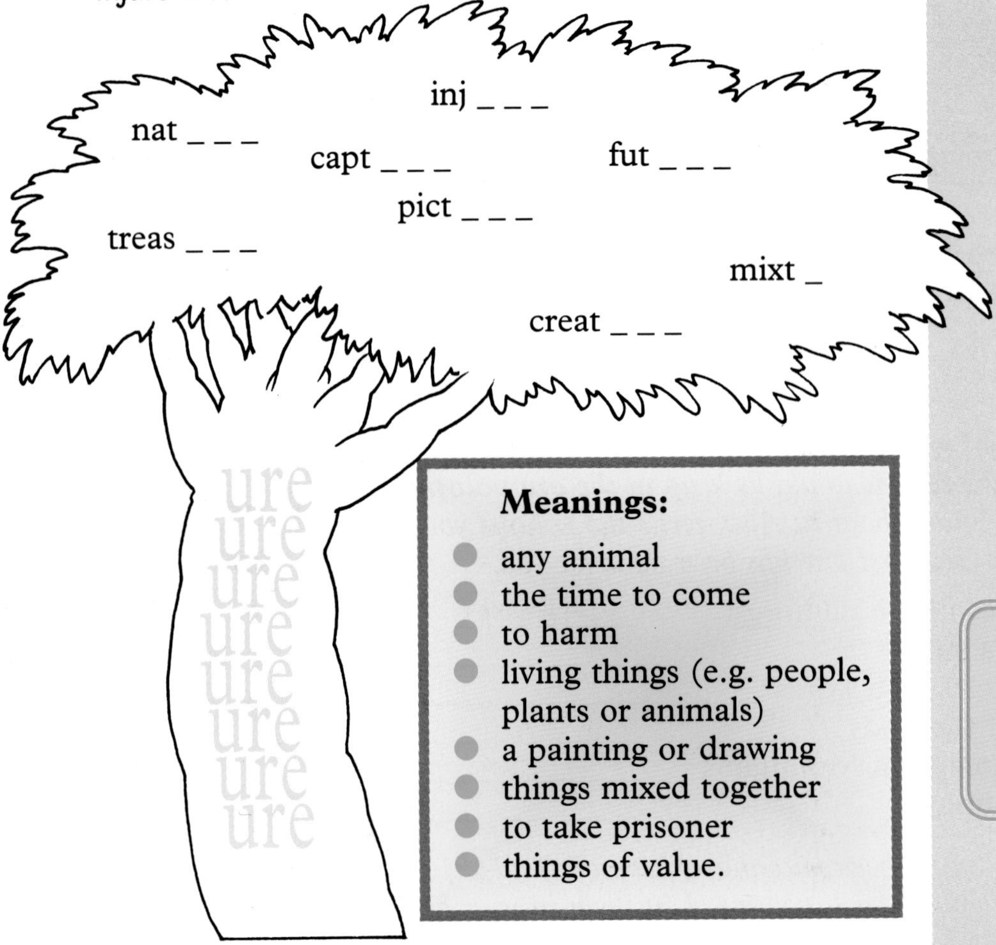

inj _ _ _

nat _ _ _

capt _ _ _   fut _ _ _

pict _ _ _

treas _ _ _

mixt _

creat _ _ _

ure ure ure ure ure ure ure ure

Meanings:
- any animal
- the time to come
- to harm
- living things (e.g. people, plants or animals)
- a painting or drawing
- things mixed together
- to take prisoner
- things of value.

extra

*Now, find the '**root**' words of these words:*
mistrust
refill
bravery
noticeable
courageous
employment
unlikely

extra

*Think of some other words ending in '**ure**'. Write them in your book.*

LANGUAGE STUDY

● Pronouns ●

Write out the passage below in your book. Choose a suitable pronoun from the box to go in each space.

Common pronouns

I	me	you	we	us		it
he	him	she	her	they		them

There was danger in the forest. Machines were cutting down all the trees. _____ were destroying everything. Jaguar was worried. '_____ must tell the other animals that _____ are in danger,' _____ said. Jaguar ran to find his friends. 'Come with _____ ,' he said. _____ all ran towards the high ground. Then the floods came. _____ washed all the soil away. But the floods also washed all the machines away. _____ smashed _____ all up. At least the machines would no longer cause _____ any harm.' _____ are saved,' the animals cried. 'But where will _____ live now?'

The prefix **'pro'** means **'in the place of'**. A **pronoun** is used **in place of a noun**. When we use a pronoun, '**The girl** went shopping' is written '**She** went shopping'.

● Alliteration ●

*Make up an alphabet of children's names. Think of at least one **alliterative adjective** for each. Write them in your book like this:*

- *Amazing Alex*
- *Big, bold Ben*

Alliteration is when the first letters of words sound the same: **R**ound and round the rugged rock, the ragged rascal ran.

Here are some ideas for the more difficult letters:

- Quiet, quizzical Quentin
- Xenophobic Xerxes
- Zany Zak

WRITING WORKSHOP

● Shape poems ●

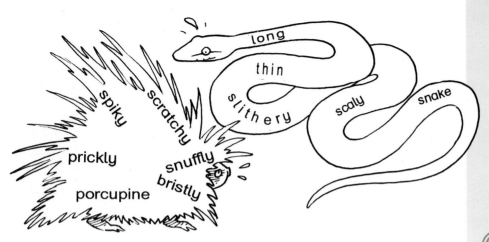

Follow these instructions to make your own **shape poem**:

- Think of a creature (like a snake, porcupine, snail, caterpillar, bat, crocodile).
- In your book, write the words that come into your head when you think about the creature. Think about how it moves, its colour, how it feels, how it sounds etc.
- Write some of the words in an outline of the creature.

● Consider the issues ●

Decide who made each statement - those in favour of cutting down rainforest trees or those against. Write the answers in your book.

The world needs the wood for timber.

The forest needs to be cleared to make room to grow coffee and bananas.

Animal habitats are destroyed.

If the forest is destroyed, we will lose the chance of discovering new plant medicines.

When the trees are cut down, the soil becomes useless.

The ranchers need room to graze their cattle.

extra

Make up some more **shape poems** *about:*

- *fireworks*
- *stars*
- *transport*
- *noises.*

extra

Write down some points **in favour** *and some points* **against** *this statement:* 'Children should be free to watch whatever TV programmes they wish.'

66

● Noah's spaceship ●

Here is an idea for a story.

Your name is Noah, and you have discovered that the Earth is going to be covered by a huge flood.

You decide to escape the flood by flying to another planet in a home-made spaceship.

You have to take along your family and other things, including different types of animals.

When you reach the planet, you have all sorts of adventures.

Now, write the story.
You will need to write about some of these things:

- how you build a spaceship
- what you will take into space
- what the journey will be like.
- if there will there be problems on board the spaceship, e.g. mess, noise, shortage of food, arguments etc.
- what happens when you arrive on the planet.

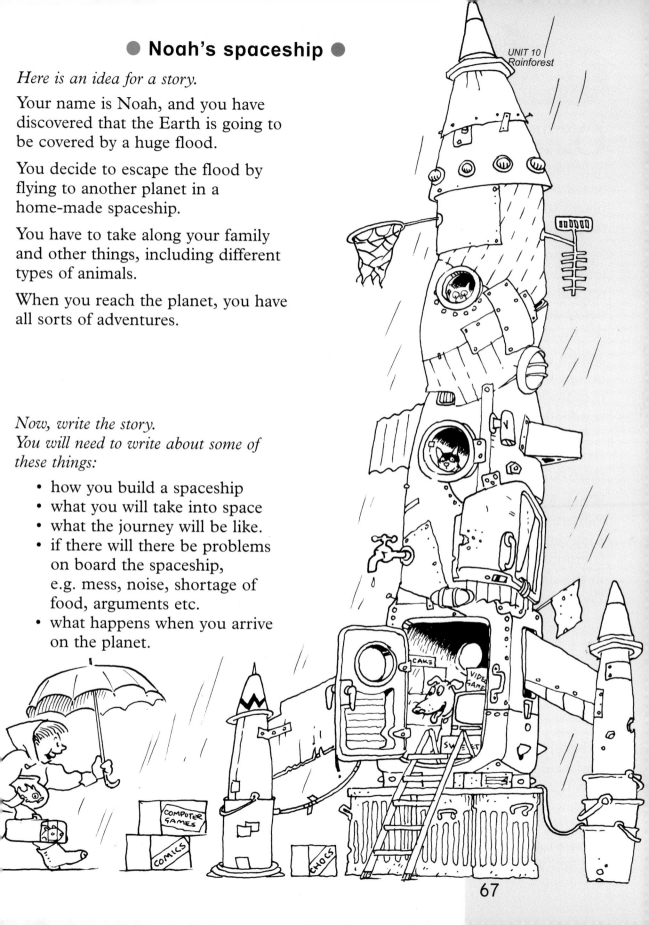

67

ON THE DAY I was born, my grandmother wrapped me in a blanket made from the wool of her sheep. She held me up in the open window, so that what I first heard was the wind. What I first saw were all the places to love: the valley, the river falling over the rocks, the hilltop where blueberries grew.

My grandfather was painting the barn, and when he saw me he cried. He carved my name- ELI - on a rafter beside his name and Grandmother's name, and the names of my papa and mama.

Mama carried me on her shoulders before I could walk, through the meadows and hay fields. The cows watched us and the sheep scattered; the dogs ran ahead, looking back with sly smiles. When the grass was high, only their tails showed.

When I was older, Papa and I plowed the fields. 'Where else is soil so sweet?' he said. Once Papa and I lay down in the field, holding hands, and the birds surrounded us: raucous black grackles, redwings, crows in the dirt that swaggered like pirates. When we left, Papa put a handful of dirt in his pocket. I did too.

Patricia MacLachlan

Think of sensible words to go in the spaces. Write them in your book.

COMPREHENSION

● Starting points ●

When I was born, my __1__ wrapped me in a __2__ blanket and held me up by the open __3__ . The first thing I heard was the __4__ . My grandfather was __5__ the barn. When he saw me, he __6__ . He carved my name on a __7__ . Before I could walk, my Mama carried me on her __8__ . When I got older, I helped Papa __9__ the fields. Papa said the soil was __10__ .

● Moving on ●

Now, answer these questions in your book.

1 Why do you think Grandfather cried when he saw Eli?

2 How can you tell that Eli has a very loving family? List the reasons.

3 What makes you think that Eli's father loves the countryside?

STUDY SKILLS

● Advantages and disadvantages ●

Draw a chart like this in your book:

Advantages	Disadvantages

• *In the '**advantages**' column, write a list of some of the things you like about the village, town or city in which you live.*

• *In the '**disadvantages**' column, write a list of the things you don't like about it.*

● Making a poster ●

I love living in Luton! I have drawn this poster to tell you all the good things about living here.

LOVELY ❀ ❀ LUTON!
✓ Close to London
✓ Good shops
✓ Plenty of parks
✓ Has an Airport
✓ Near the motorway
❀ ❀

Now, draw a poster to tell people all the good things about where you live.

ⓘ Follow these instructions to draw your poster:

1 Draw your poster in rough first.

2 Cross out anything you don't like.

3 Check your spellings.

4 Make sure the information fits nicely in the space.

5 When you are happy with your poster, draw it out neatly and colour it.

WORD STUDY

● Homophones ●

Copy these sentences into your book. Ring the correct word to complete each one.

1 The girl had <u>fair/fare</u> hair.

2 I got very <u>board/bored</u> with the journey.

3 I <u>herd/heard</u> a noise in the middle of the night.

4 My aunt said I had <u>grown/groan</u> up a lot.

5 The children got <u>their/there</u> shirts very dirty.

6 The greedy dog ate the <u>hole/whole</u> tin of food.

7 The train sped <u>threw/through</u> the tunnel.

8 May I please have a <u>piece/peace</u> of chocolate?

> **Homophones** are words that sound alike but have different meanings, like '**here**' and '**hear**'. If you're not sure which word to use, look them both up in a dictionary.

● Rhyming words ●

 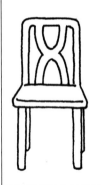  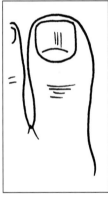

sweet   seat   snow   toe

Match each word in **Box A** *to a word that* **rhymes** *with it, in* **Box B**. *Write the pairs of words in your book like this:*

1 date - great

A card   pair   date   brain   stay
      clean   coal   purse   thumb   cried

B prey   sighed   verse   plane   great
      machine   wear   guard   come   bowl

70

LANGUAGE STUDY

● Things grown-ups say! ●

In your book, write what you think these sayings mean.

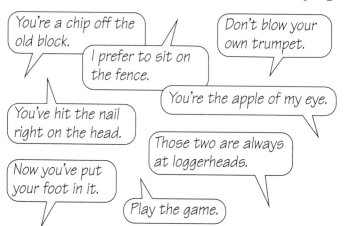

You're a chip off the old block.

I prefer to sit on the fence.

Don't blow your own trumpet.

You've hit the nail right on the head.

You're the apple of my eye.

Those two are always at loggerheads.

Now you've put your foot in it.

Play the game.

Where else is soil so sweet?

● Comparing adjectives ●

Why can't we say beautiful, beautifuller, beautifullest?

beautiful

more beautiful

most beautiful

Copy and complete this chart in your book.

Adjective	Comparative form of adjective	Superlative form of adjective
beautiful	*more beautiful*	*most beautiful*
comfortable		
generous		
handsome		
ignorant		
famous		
wonderful		
miserable		

When we are comparing things using **long adjectives**, we can't add '**er**' and '**est**' endings. They don't look or sound right!

71

WRITING WORKSHOP

● Conjunctions ●

Copy these sentences into your book. Choose the correct **conjunction** *to complete each one.*

1 The man ate a sandwich (before/since) he rowed to the island.

2 You wait here (while/until) it's time to go home.

3 I know it's your fault (because/so) I saw you do it.

4 Let me know (if/as) you want to come to my party.

5 He stayed still (and/as) he had been ordered.

6 She read a book (unless/while) I watched TV.

7 I can come (while/whenever) you want me to.

8 You can't go (unless/since) I can come too.

● Punctuation ●

Rewrite this letter in your book. Add punctuation marks in the correct places.

I'm staying with Uncle John for the holidays. I keep trying to write a letter to my mum and dad, but I can't get it right. Can you help me?

white horse farm
canterbury rd
ashford
kent

25 october 1998

dear mum and dad

im having a lovely time at uncle johns farm its great feeding the animals i love the horses theres one called silver hes my favourite he lets me brush him on wednesday were going to the shops in dover ill write again soon

Love

Sam

extra

Imagine that you are on holiday somewhere nice. Write a letter to your best friend, and tell them about some of the things you have seen and done.

72

● My very own special place ●

Think of a place that is very special to you. In your book, write why it means so much to you, like this.

> I love my bedroom. It's a place where I can be on my own. I can listen to music or read quietly. I love the time just before I go to sleep. I can lie in my bed and think about the day's events and what I'll do tomorrow. I can hear the TV downstairs and the murmur of voices as I drift off to sleep.

● Memories ●

I remember when I learned to ride my bike.

I'll never forget the day my dog died.

What special memories do you have? Write about two of them. You could write about:
- *your earliest memory*
- *your happiest memory*
- *an exciting memory*
- *a sad memory*
- *when you first learned to do something special*
- *what you remember about a very special relative.*

73

1 Pirate and merchant ships

IN THE 17th and 18th centuries, merchants and traders brought valuable cargoes of gold, silk and other goods from Europe by ship. These ships were heavy and slow, and were not usually well-armed. They were easy prey for pirates who sailed in smaller, faster ships.

2 _____

WHEN PIRATES attacked merchant ships, they fired cannons and flew their flag, which had either a skeleton or a skull and crossbones on it. As the pirate ship pulled alongside the merchant ship, the pirates jumped aboard it, waving their cutlasses, firing pistols and shouting.

3 _____

PIRATES WERE often criminals running away from the law, sailors from the Navy who had been captured or adventurers out to make their fortune. If caught, they were usually hanged.

> Read **Treasure Island** by R. L. Stevenson to find out more about pirates.

4 _____

CAPTAIN KIDD was one of the most infamous pirates. He was captured and hanged in 1701. Edward Teach, or Blackbeard as he was better known, stuck pieces of burning rope into his beard when going into battle to make him look even more fearsome. There were even women pirates. Two of the best known women pirates were Anne Bonny and Mary Read.

COMPREHENSION

● Starting points ●

Answer these questions in your book.

1 What sort of goods did merchants carry on their ships?

2 Why were merchant ships 'easy prey' for pirates?

3 What might pirate's flags have on them?

4 What three types of people often became pirates? Name them.

5 What happened to Captain Kidd?

6 What was unusual about Edward Teach?

extra

Try to find out something about each of these pirates:
- Calico Jack Rackham
- Henry Every
- Bartholomew Roberts
- Edward Teach
- Captain Kidd.

● Moving on ●

Now, write the answers to these questions in your book.

1 Do you think being a pirate was exciting?
   Explain your answer.

2 What do these words mean?
   Look them up in a dictionary if you are not sure.
   a) cargoes **b)** cutlass **c)** criminals

3 What do you think pirates were like? Were they brave
   or just greedy? Explain your answer.

4 Did it surprise you to learn that there were women
   pirates? Explain your answer.

Look at the four
paragraphs opposite.
Paragraph 1 has been
given a **title**. The **title**
tells you what the **main**
idea of the **paragraph** is.

STUDY SKILLS

● Main ideas ●

*Think of good **titles** for **paragraphs** 2, 3 and 4
and write them in your book.*

● Paragraphs ●

*In your book, write a **paragraph** to go with each of these titles:*
1 Flags **2** Sweets **3** Life at School

● Making notes ●

*Copy out this **paragraph**. Underline the words that you think
are important.*

> Life at sea was <u>hard</u> and <u>dangerous</u>. One slip when climbing
> the rigging of the ship could mean falling to your death.
> Living space was cramped and unhealthy.
> For punishment, a pirate could be flogged with a 'cat o' nine
> tails' (a whip with nine cords). Food on board ship was awful.
> Fresh fruit and vegetables rotted, so pirates ate mostly dried
> fish and salted meat. Biscuits and flour soon became full
> of wriggling maggots.

extra

Here are some
facts (in note
form) about Sir
John Hawkins.
Use them to write
a paragraph
about this famous
sailor.

- born 1532, Plymouth
- from a seafaring family
- joined the Navy
- went on many voyages
- improved the design of galleons
- 1588 - fought the Spanish
- knighted for bravery
- 1595 - sailed with Francis Drake
- died on board ship
- buried at sea

WORD STUDY

● 'au' or 'ui' ●

*Copy and complete these words with either **'au'** or **'ui'**.*

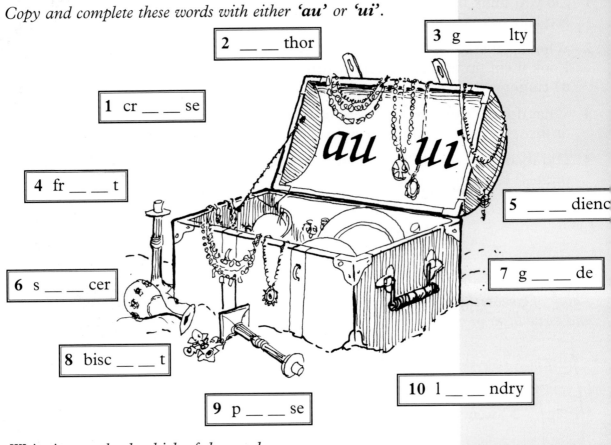

2 __ __ thor

3 g __ __ lty

1 cr __ __ se

au ui

4 fr __ __ t

5 __ __ dienc

6 s __ __ cer

7 g __ __ de

8 bisc __ __ t

10 l __ __ ndry

9 p __ __ se

Write in your book which of the words mean:

1 Someone who writes books.

2 A crowd of people who are
   watching something.

3 A place where washing is done.

4 To stop for a while.

5 You put a cup on this.

Now, write the
meanings of the
'ui' words.

extra

*Think of some
more **'au'** and
'ui' words.
Write them in
your book.*

76

LANGUAGE STUDY

● Prepositions ●

*Write six sentences in your book. Use some **prepositions** from the box below in them. Do it like this:*

Blackbeard stuck pieces of burning rope <u>into</u> his beard to scare people.

behind	into	off	above	towards
near	down	between	through	over

> A **preposition** tells you the **position** of one thing to another.

● Adverbs of manner ●

*Copy these sentences into your book. Circle the **verb** and underline the **adverb** in each one. The first one has been done for you.*

1 The girl (ran) home <u>quickly</u>.

2 The stray dog barked loudly.

3 The wheels on the bike squeaked noisily.

4 I looked longingly at the ice cream.

5 Slowly, I returned home.

How did Blackbeard glare?

Blackbeard glared <u>fiercely</u>.

● Adverbs of time ●

*Copy and complete these sentences using '**adverbs of time**' from the box.*

soon	never	now	later	sometimes

> 'Adverbs of manner' tell us how a **verb happens**. They mostly end in 'ly'.

1 The sun is shining _____ .

2 _____ it will be time for bed.

3 I _____ play with matches.

4 I'll see you _____ .

5 _____, I have a lolly.

When did you have a cold?

Yesterday, I had a cold.

> 'Adverbs of time' tell us **when** an action took place.

77

WRITING WORKSHOP

● Punctuation ●

Rewrite these jokes with the correct punctuation.

Question: whats small white round and smells terrible
Answer: its a ping pong ball

Captain: why didnt you stop the ball
Goalkeeper: i thought thats what the net was for

Question: why is tennis such a noisy game
Answer: because theres always a racket

Child: why do you wear two pairs of socks
Golfer: in case i get a hole in one

Ho! Ho! Ho!

Pirates are good at telling jokes,
but they are no good at punctuation!

● A pirate's curse ●

*Draw a chart like this in your book, and make up some more
pirate's curses.*

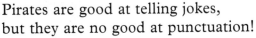

May your	noun	be	verb	by a	adjective	noun
May your	sword	be	swallowed	by a	ferocious	shark.
May your	bike	be	squashed	by a	giant	boulder.
May your	lunch	be	grabbed	by a	hairy	gorilla.

extra

Imagine that you are a pirate called either Peg Leg Jake or Black Eye Bess. Write a diary of your life on board the good ship 'Skull Duggery' for a week.

● Mystery Island ●

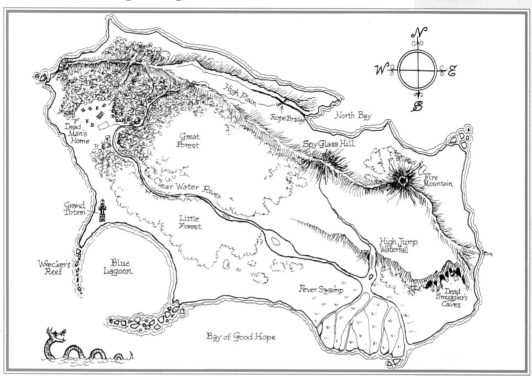

Choose one of these ideas to write about.

1 The splintering sound of wood being ripped apart filled the air. The wind shrieked as the ship was hurled against the reef. Huge waves pounded it without mercy. Suddenly, you are thrown into the raging sea, and swept towards Mystery Island...
Write what happens next.

2 Mystery Island is a deserted island. Choose ten things you would take along with you if you were sent to live there. Write down your reason for taking each thing.

3 You are an explorer who has travelled to Mystery Island in search of adventure. Write an account of some of your journeys around the island. Describe some of the things you discover, and draw some sketches of the more unusual things (including plants and animals). Remember to label your drawings.

4 Imagine that you are shipwrecked on Mystery Island. You have no food or shelter, and no tools except a knife. Write some instructions for how you would do these things:
• catch something to eat
• make a fire
• build a shelter
• make a comfortable bed.

The capture of Aslan — Unit 13

'STOP!' said the Witch. 'Let him first be shaved.' Another roar of mean laughter went up from her followers as an ogre with a pair of shears came forward and squatted down by Aslan's head. Snip-snip-snip went the shears, and masses of curling gold began to fall to the ground. Then the ogre stood back, and the children, watching from their hiding place, could see the face of Aslan looking all small and different without its mane. The enemies also saw the difference. 'Why, he's only a great cat after all!' cried one. 'Is that what we were afraid of?' said another. And they surged round Aslan, jeering at him, saying things like, 'Puss, Puss! Poor Pussy!' and 'How many mice have you caught today, Cat?' and 'Would you like a saucer of milk, Pussums?' 'Oh, how can they?' said Lucy, tears streaming down her cheeks. 'The brutes! The brutes!' For now that the first shock was over, the shorn face of Aslan looked to her braver, and more beautiful, and more patient than ever. 'Muzzle him!' said the Witch. And even now, as they worked about his face putting on the muzzle, one bite from his jaws would have cost two or three of them their hands. But he never moved. And this seemed to enrage all that rabble. Everyone was at him now. Those who had been afraid to come near him, even after he was bound, began to find their courage, and for a few minutes the two girls could not even see him - so thickly was he surrounded by the whole crowd of creatures kicking him, hitting him, spitting on him, jeering at him. *C. S. Lewis*

Write answers to these questions in your book.

COMPREHENSION

● Starting points ●

1 Who ordered Aslan to be shorn?

2 What did the ogre use to cut Aslan's hair?

3 Who was watching from a hiding place?

4 Why did they muzzle Aslan?

5 How did Aslan react to being jeered at?

6 How did the crowd treat Aslan?

extra

Find out what happened next by reading The Lion, the Witch and the Wardrobe by C. S. Lewis.

● Moving on ●

Now, answer these questions in your book.

1 What kind of animal is Aslan? How do you know this?

2 Did Aslan look different without his mane? In what ways did he look different?

3 How do you think the girls felt as they watched Aslan being shorn?

STUDY SKILLS

● Using a thesaurus ●

*Here is what a **thesaurus** says about the word '**courage**'.*

key word   part of speech (*n* = noun)   words with a similar meaning

courage *n.* valour, gallantry, fearlessness, bravery

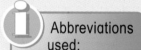

A thesaurus tells you which words have a similar meaning. It is set out rather like a dictionary.

1 In your book:
   a) write whether '**courage**' is an **adjective, adverb, verb** or **noun**
   b) write two words you could use instead of 'courage'.

*Here are some more **thesaurus** entries:*

navigate *v.* direct, sail, steer
navy *n.* fleet, shipping, vessels, ships
near *adj.* close, nearby, adjacent, neighbouring
nearly *adv.* approximately, closely, almost

Abbreviations used:
- *adj.* = adjective
- *adv.* = adverb
- *n.* = noun
- *v.* = verb

In your book, write the full form of the abbreviation that goes in each space. The first one has been done for you.

2 **a)** navigate is a _____verb_____
   b) navy is a _____
   c) near is an _____
   d) nearly is an _____

Now, write the answers to these questions in your book.

3 **a)** What five-letter word means 'navigate'?
   b) What word beginning with 'f' means 'navy'?
   c) What does 'approximately' mean?

extra

*Use a **thesaurus** to find words that have a similar meaning to:*
   - *jeer*
   - *brute*
   - *rabble*
   - *ogre*

WORD STUDY

● Using the prefixes 'en' and 'ex' ●

*Decide whether the **prefix 'en'** or **'ex'** should go in front of each of the word endings. Write the completed words in your book.*

1 ☐ courage   2 ☐ pect   3 ☐ port

4 ☐ rage   5 ☐ able   6 ☐ change

7 ☐ dear   8 ☐ plain   9 ☐ pand

10 ☐ force   11 ☐ claim   12 ☐ rich

Write six sentences in your book. Use some of the 'en' and 'ex' words that you have made in them.

● Three of a kind ●

Find the sets of three words that go together. Write them in your book like this:

muzzle, puzzle, guzzle.

muzzle	rabble	fiddle
snuffle	wiggle	rattle
giggle	cattle	dabble
puzzle	muffle	riddle
battle	gabble	guzzle
twiddle	wriggle	scuffle

extra

Think of some words that end in:

-azzle
-izzle
-affle
-uddle
-ittle
-ettle

List them in your book.

82

LANGUAGE STUDY

● Making subjects and verbs match ●

Think of a **suitable** *subject to go in each space. Write the completed sentences in your book.*

1 _____ bark.
2 _____ hop.
3 _____ were dancing.
4 _____ were eating.

Now, complete each of these sentences with a suitable subject.

1 _____ barks.
2 _____ hops.
3 _____ was dancing.
4 _____ was eating.

Rewrite these sentences correctly in your book.

Each underlined **verb** *should be changed to match the* **subject** *of the sentence.*

1 The man <u>are</u> eating an apple.

2 We <u>was</u> walking home when it rained.

3 My brother <u>done</u> his homework last night.

4 Where <u>is</u> you going?

5 Squirrels <u>collects</u> nuts in the autumn.

6 An owl <u>come</u> out when it is dark.

> **i** The **subject** of a sentence is who or what does things:
>
> The **dog** eats a bone.
>
> **Doctors** care for me.
>
> The **subject** and **verb** in a sentence must always match. If the **subject** is **singular**, the **verb** must be **singular**. If the **subject** is **plural**, the **verb** must be **plural**.

● Synonyms ●

Rewrite these sentences. In each, replace the word **'went'** *with another suitable word, like this:*
  The train **went** *through the tunnel.*
  The train **thundered** *through the tunnel.*

1 The worm went through the grass.

2 The horse went round the track.

3 The woman went into the shop.

4 The duck went across the lane.

5 The ape went from tree to tree.

6 The boy went into the swimming pool.

> **i** **Synonyms** are words with **similar meanings**. You can use a **thesaurus** to look for **synonyms**.

> **extra**
> *How many different words can you think of that mean to 'speak'?*

WRITING WORKSHOP

● Writing a play ●

In your book, write out the story in the form of a play. Some parts of it have already been done for you.

CHARACTERS: *Jake and Jenny* (the bullies),
Tom (the victim) *Captain Lion Heart* (the rescuer)
Narrator

Narrator: Little Tom was out playing, when the two local bullies, Jake and Jenny, trapped him.

Jake: Just look! Here's Tiny Tom.

Jenny: _____

Tom: _____

Jenny: Oh! The little man's got a tongue!

Jake: _____

Tom: _____

Narrator: Suddenly, there was a flash of smoke and there stood Captain Lion Heart.

Jake: _____

Jenny: _____

Tom: _____

Captain Lion Heart: _____

Now, write what you think Captain Lion Heart did next.

extra

Write what you think the purpose of the narrator is.

● Being teased ●

I get teased because I wear glasses.

I get teased because I have freckles.

I get teased because I stutter.

I get teased because I don't have the right trainers.

Write about a time when you were teased. Say:

•   what happened

•   how you felt when you were being teased.

Now, write some things you could do to stop someone from being teased.

● Diary of a good day ●

23 Thursday

I knew it was going to be a good day when I woke up. The sun was streaming through the window. When I got downstairs, my breakfast was ready. I was surprised when John and Shiva called for me because I had fallen out with them yesterday. We joked about school.

Mrs Jones said that my reading was lots better, and I got every sum right. There were chips for dinner, and we had Art, my favourite lesson, in the afternoon. When I got home, Mum told me about the holiday we were going on next week, and she let me stay up half an hour later than usual. Today has been a very good day!

Write about either:
- your best day ever   OR   *- your worst day ever.*

---

extra

In your book, write one nice thing you could say:

- *to a friend*
- *to someone who doesn't like you*
- *to someone at home*

THE Nurgla was very, very old, and very, very tired, and he looked as old and tired as he felt. His small head was wrinkled and lined with age; the leathery horns which sprouted from the top of his forehead were crumpled and creased; and an untidy fringe of green, seaweed-like hair hung over his eyebrows and sometimes made him furious because it got in his eyes. Two large nostrils flared in the folds of his craggy cheeks, and dreadful sharp teeth jutted out from his huge jaws. A ridge of jagged spikes ran the length of the Nurgla's long, long neck, down the spine of his enormous body, right to the tip of his scaly tail. To complete the horrible picture, his round body was covered in hard, overlapping, armour-like plates, and his vast flippers were an unbelievable size eighteen. In short, the Nurgla was hideous.

He had frightened people out of their wits since the beginning of time - and to be perfectly honest, he enjoyed his fearsome reputation. It made him feel strong and powerful when people ran away from him in terror. Every summer he spent his holidays in a lake in Scotland, and whenever he rose from the water to browse along the shore where his favourite weeds grew, thick and luscious, his dreadful appearance spread fear throughout the length and breadth of the land.

Harry Secombe

COMPREHENSION

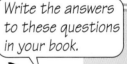

Write the answers to these questions in your book.

● Starting points ●

1 What did the Nurgla look like? Describe his:
   a) head **b)** hair **c)** body

2 For how long had the Nurgla frightened people?

3 What did he like to eat?

● Moving on ●

Now, answer these questions in your book.

1 Do you think the Nurgla was a nasty creature? Explain your answer.

2 What do you think the word 'reputation' means? (Look it up in a dictionary if you are not sure.)

3 What do you think is the most attractive animal? What is the ugliest one? Give reasons for your answers.

extra

Draw the Nurgla, and make up some labels to describe his different features.

STUDY SKILLS

● Word association ●

Copy this chart into your book.
For each row of words, underline
the words that you **associate**
with the first word.
The first one has been done for you.

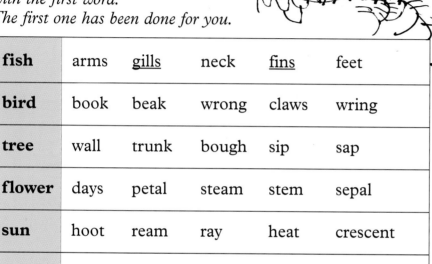

Which of these
words do you
associate with me:
honey, horns, weeds,
skates, spikes?

fish	arms	gills	neck	fins	feet
bird	book	beak	wrong	claws	wring
tree	wall	trunk	bough	sip	sap
flower	days	petal	steam	stem	sepal
sun	hoot	ream	ray	heat	crescent
water	tip	steam	wet	surface	evaporate

If you are not
sure about
what any of the
words mean, look
them up in a
dictionary.

● Analogies ●

Copy and complete these analogies in your book. The first one
has been done for you.

1 Wrist is to arm, as ankle is to ___leg___ .

2 _____ are to birds, as scales are to fish.

3 Hearing is to ear, as _____ is to eyes.

4 _____ is to water, as smoke is to fire.

5 Tear is to sorrow, as smile is to _____ .

6 Nose is to smell, as _____ is to taste.

7 Food is to hunger, as drink is to _____ .

8 Statue is to sculptor, as book is to _____ .

WORD STUDY

● Proofreading for spelling mistakes ●

*There are **18** spelling mistakes in this piece of writing about the Nurgla. Find the words that are wrong. In your book, rewrite each word correctly.*

FIRST WITH THE NEWS

The CARDIGAN

BOFFIN IN MERCY DASH

The Nurgla is coming!

'Nothing to worry about', says local councillor

Panic spreads as local people flee the Nurgla

Police call for calm as Nurgla expert flies in from Scotland

MANY people have been fritened by the Nurgla. His apperance is dreadfull.

His small head is very rinkled. He has two horns sprowting from his forhead. A frinje of green hair hangs over his eyebrowes. A ridge of jaged spickes runs down his neck. His enormus boddy is coverd in plates like armor. The Nurgla's feet are an unbeleivable size aighteen! The Nurgla is a really hidious creature.

In the summer, he can be found in a lake in Scotland. He likes to eat weads that grow by the lake.

LANGUAGE STUDY

● Sound words ●

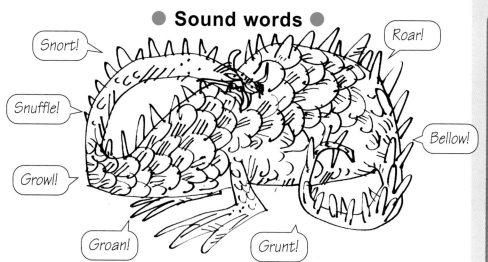

Choose suitable words from the box to describe the noises made by these creatures. Write the completed sentences in your book.

1 Pigeons _____ .   2 Turkeys _____ .

3 Sheep _____ .   4 Pigs _____ .

5 Parrots _____ .   6 Owls_____ .

7 Hens _____ .   8 Donkeys _____ .

9 Elephants _____ .   10 Bears _____ .

● Diminutives ●

Copy these lists in to your book. Match each parent to its young.
The first one has been done for you.

cat	cub
pig	foal
deer	piglet
cow	gosling
dog	tadpole
fox	fawn
goose	lamb
sheep	calf
frog	puppy
horse	kitten

growl
bray
trumpet
cackle
hiss
cluck
whinny
hoot
scream
screech
grunt
coo
squeal
bleat
crow
gobble
howl
snarl

89

WRITING WORKSHOP

● Using descriptive language ●

Artists paint pictures to tell you things.

Authors use words to paint pictures for you.

Read the passage about the Nurgla (on page 86) again. Now, complete this work in your book.

1   How well do you think the author has described (or 'painted a picture' of) the Nurgla for you? Write some sentences that say what you like about his writing. Is there anything you don't like?

2   The author has tried to use interesting words and phrases in the description. Write down five that you particularly liked.

● Playing with words ●

The Nurgla's horns were <u>cr</u>umpled and <u>cr</u>eased.

Follow these instructions to make up your own poem:

*   Choose an animal. (It can be a real or make-believe.)

*   Choose four letters of the alphabet.

*   Think of two **'describing words' (adjectives)** beginning with each letter.

*   Write them in your book in the same way as above.

extra

*Make up a second verse for your poem. Think of '**describing words**' that begin with four different letters.*

90

● Nice or nasty?

The Snitter   The Glugcrump

- Choose one of the imaginary creatures above.

- Decide whether it is going to be **nice** or **nasty**.

- Write a description of it in your book. (Remember to use some interesting descriptive words and phrases.) The ideas below should help you to write your description.

1   Write about its **appearance**. Describe its:
    - eyes, mouth, nose, ears, chin, hair etc.
    - size, shape, colour, texture, arms, legs, claws, tail etc.

2   Describe:

   -**its habitat**. Does it live in a cave, marsh, sea, wood, lake?
   -**how it moves**. Does it plod, leap, hop etc.?
   -**what noises it makes**. Does it howl, sigh, whisper, roar etc.?
   -**what it eats**. Does it eat small children, teachers, cotton wool, seaweed etc.?

ⓘ The sort of creature that you choose to write about (**nice** or **nasty**) will affect the words you use to describe it.

Do you remember?   Test 3

STUDY SKILLS

1 *Imagine that some important visitors came to your school. In your book, write five good things you would tell them about the school. Then, write two things you would not tell them!*

2 *Use these notes to help you write a few sentences.*

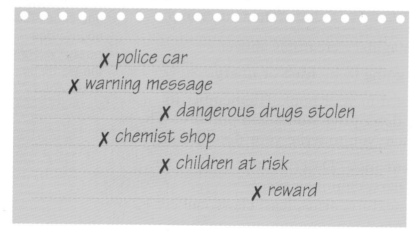

✗ police car
✗ warning message
    ✗ dangerous drugs stolen
✗ chemist shop
    ✗ children at risk
      ✗ reward

WORD STUDY

In your book, write three words:

1 ending in '**-ure**'.

2 beginning with the prefixes '**en**' and '**ex**'.

LANGUAGE STUDY

*Copy and complete these sentences with suitable **pronouns**.*

1 a) The lady was on her way to Oxford, but
she lost _____ way.

b) Sweets are bad for you, so you should not eat too
many of _____ .

c) My friend and I went home, and
then _____ watched TV.

*In your book, write sentences that contain these '**adverbs of manner**':*

2 a) bravely   **b)** brightly   **c)** fairly

*Now, write sentences that contain these '**adverbs of time**':*

3 a) soon   **b)** always   **c)** never

4 *Write five other words you could use instead of 'nice' in this sentence:*

It was a nice day.

WRITING WORKSHOP

Punctuate this passage correctly in your book.

in the garden a mysterious dark figure
was trying to get in the front window
the police car stopped quietly two
police officers got out crept up the path
slowly and grabbed the woman what do
you think youre doing one of the
policemen said dont worry officer im
not breaking in ive just forgotten my
front door key the lady replied

IDEAS FOR STORY STARTERS

Sometimes, I find it really hard to start stories. Here are just a few starter ideas for stories to help you begin writing.

Theme	Situation
Accidents	While playing? In the kitchen? In the science laboratory? Somewhere else?
Trapped	In an old building that collapses? While exploring underwater? In a fire? Somewhere else ?
Kidnapped	By robbers? By pirates? By spies? By someone else?
Disasters	Fire? Flood? Gale? Tidal wave? Earthquake? Avalanche? Something else?
Burglars	At home? At school? In the bank? Somewhere else?
The Object	Someone discovers a mysterious object? What powers does it have? What happens ?
The Time Machine	Adventures in other ages - back to the Cavemen, Egyptians, Romans, Fire of London - or into the future?
UFOs	Strange aliens from outer space land on Earth? You land on an unknown planet? Something else?
The Strange Drink	You drink a magic potion and shrink, grow very tall, become very brainy? Something else happens?

IDEAS FOR CHECKING AND EDITING STORIES

Characters
- Have you described how they look, feel, behave?

Settings
- Have you described the setting well enough?

Story plot
- Does your story have a good beginning, middle, end?
- Can you make it more interesting?
- Do you need to add or move anything?

Punctuation
- Do all your sentences make sense?
- Have you checked your punctuation for: capital letters, full stops, commas, question and exclamation marks, speech marks?

Spelling and handwriting
- Have you checked for silly spelling mistakes?
- Is your handwriting clear and easy to read?

Presentation
- Are you going to print your story on the computer?
- Are you going to illustrate it?
- What format will you present your story in: exercise book, paper, booklet, some other way?